MASTERING AP MODERN WORLD HISTORY

A Practice Book for Students (by Teachers)

Chris Peek, Kate Nocca
and Lauren Ortega

Copyright © 2019 Peek Learning Consultants. All rights reserved.

Permission is given for individual classroom teachers to reproduce the pages for classroom use. Reproduction of these materials for an entire school system is strictly forbidden.

For permission to reuse material for all other purposes, please contact the authors at PeekLearningConsultants@gmail.com.

Limit of Liability/Disclaimer of Warranty: While the authors have used their best efforts in preparing this book, they make no representations or warranties with respect to the accuracy or completeness of the contents of this book and specifically disclaim any implied warranties or merchantability or fitness for a particular purpose. No warranty may be created or extended by sales representatives or written sales materials. The advice, strategies and materials contained herein may not be suitable for your situation. You should consult with a professional where appropriate. The authors shall not be liable for any loss of profit or any other commercial damages, including but not limited to special, incidental, consequential, or other damages. Readers should be aware that the AP World History course changes periodically and the exam requirements and related skills may have changed between the time this was written and when it is read.

AP and Advanced Placement Program are registered trademarks of the College Board, which is not affiliated with the authors. The ideas and opinions expressed in this book belong solely to the authors, and are neither endorsed by nor intended to represent the College Board.

ISBN-13: 9781688767683

THE AUTHORS

Combined, the authors have over 70 years of teaching experience, and over 30 years of teaching AP World History. They have also amassed over 25 years of invaluable participation as readers and leaders of the AP World History exam. Working together at a socially, culturally, and economically diverse 6A Title I school in the Greater Houston area, they built a program which has seen a consistently high level of success.

Chris Peek has been involved with AP World History since its inception. Although he has retired from the classroom, he continues to work as a consultant with the College Board. Chris has written exams for major publishing houses as well as questions for the TExES exam for teacher certification. Chris attempts to keep Kate on a steady course as she sometimes veers in tangential directions.

Kate Nocca, born in England, has a long history of international education, eventually finding her way to Houston, Texas, where she has worked for many years. Kate has been instrumental in the development of the AP World History curriculum for Houston ISD. She has written exam questions for a major publishing house and has participated in question writing for an on-line review. Kate is never satisfied and often edits her own edits.

Lauren Ortega, although fairly new to the team, has proven invaluable with her grasp of history, technical expertise, and editing abilities. Without her help, you would not understand a word written in this skills guide.

To organize a one, two, or three day training session on world history writing, contact the authors at PeekLearningConsultants@gmail.com.

CONTENTS

The Authors iii

Acknowledgments 2

How to Use This Practice Book 3

Multiple-Choice (MC) Tests 4

    MC Directions 5

    MC Test 1: 1200 to 1600 6

    MC Test 2: 1200 to 2001 30

    MC Test 3: 1200 to 2001 50

Short-Answer Questions (SAQ) 78

    SAQ Directions 79

    SAQ Set 1: 1200 to 1450 80

    SAQ Set 2: 1450 to 1750 83

    SAQ Set 3: 1750 to 1900 87

    SAQ Set 4: 1900 to 2001 90

Document-Based Questions (DBQs) 94

    DBQ Directions 95

    DBQ 1: 1200 to 1550 96

    DBQ 2: 1400 to 1750 100

    DBQ 3: 1880 to 1920 104

    DBQ 4: 20th Century 108

    DBQ 5: 20th Century 112

Long Essay Questions (LEQs) 116

    LEQ Directions 117

    LEQ Set 1: Social Structures 118

    LEQ Set 2: Networks of Exchange 119

    LEQ Set 3: States and Empires 120

    LEQ Set 4: The Environment 121

ANSWER KEY 122

- MC Test 1 123
- MC Test 2 130
- MC Test 3 136
- SAQ Set 1 142
- SAQ Set 2 146
- SAQ Set 3 150
- SAQ Set 4 154
- DBQ Grading Rubric 158
- DBQ 1 159
- DBQ 2 161
- DBQ 3 163
- DBQ 4 165
- DBQ 5 167
- LEQ Grading Rubric 169
- LEQ 1A 170
- LEQ 1B 171
- LEQ 1C 172
- LEQ 2A 173
- LEQ 2B 174
- LEQ 2C 175
- LEQ 3A 176
- LEQ 3B 177
- LEQ 3C 178
- LEQ 4A 179
- LEQ 4B 180
- LEQ 4C 181

ACKNOWLEDGMENTS

We want to thank the more than 4,000 students who have gone through our AP World History program over the years. Their insight, hard work, good humor, and dedication to learning keeps us going. We'd especially like to thank the students who volunteered their own time to write sample responses for this book— Eunice Bao, Aiden Berwick, Sarah Birenbaum, Lucy Ding, Laura Hester, Ioana Nechiti, Eli Pustilnik, Kevin Wang, and Kat Wong—you're amazing and we can't thank you enough!

HOW TO USE THIS PRACTICE BOOK

This book is packed with practice exercises for all components of the AP World History: Modern exam. Through dedicated use of this book, your knowledge of world history, your grasp of historical thinking skills, and your overall confidence in test-taking will improve.

The biggest mistake students make is to delay test preparation until a month before the exam—all that cramming only leads to confusion and stress. To get the maximum benefits from your test preparation, you should begin preparing seriously for the exam at least four months before your test date. The exercises in this book cover every period of the course, and are in chronological order. Therefore, even if you have not fully completed the course, you can still practice the exam skills using practice sets that are testing content from the earlier time periods.

We strongly advise you to NOT complete a full-length practice exam (all 3 hours and 15 minutes of it) in one sitting. That will do nothing but exhaust you. You do not need to experience that more than once! What you should do instead is to practice each component individually. As long as you limit yourself to the same time restrictions you will face in the national exam (55 minutes for the MC test, 40 minutes for the SAQ, 60 minutes for DBQ, 40 minutes for LEQ), you will be prepared to handle the time restrictions on test day. For example, set aside an hour one afternoon to practice the DBQ. A few days later, set aside 40 minutes to practice the LEQ, and so on. Spacing out your practice will keep the skills fresh and ensures you get the most out of it.

Best of luck to you, and congratulations on your commitment to doing well! Remember to consult the answer key in the back. And if you still have lingering questions on the content or skills, be sure to ask your world history teacher.

MULTIPLE-CHOICE QUESTIONS

MC Directions:

The multiple-choice (MC) section of the test consists of 55 questions and accounts for 40% of your total exam score. This section contains three practice multiple-choice tests. The first test covers material typically learned in the first half of the course (up to 1600). This is designed so that you do not have to wait until the end of the year to begin practicing multiple-choice questions. The other two tests in the section cover the entire course, from 1200 to 2001, featuring questions from each time period in the same proportion as the national exam.

In order to prepare for the exam, it is best to replicate exam conditions whenever you practice. Just like with every other section of the test, learning to work under the time constraint is crucial for success. For the MC test, the time limit is 55 minutes, or one minute per question.

When you are finished, check your answers using the key in the back, which includes explanations of the reasoning behind each correct answer.

COMMON MISTAKES	WHAT TO DO INSTEAD
misunderstanding the question	Read each question at least twice, and don't be afraid to underline key words. The questions often contain key words that, if missed, can set you up for disaster. For example, a question might ask for a *long-term* result of something, but if you breeze through the question and miss it, you might mistakenly pick a *short-term* effect that was provided as an answer option. There are often answer choices provided that are true statements in and of themselves, but that doesn't mean they're the correct choice!
misinterpreting the stimulus	Make sure to read the attribution. There are often important details that will help you better understand the stimulus and put it into context. Review the stimulus more than once—do it before you read any of the questions, and again after reading the questions.

MC Test 1: 1200 to 1600

Questions 1-3 refer to the passage below.

The early Song leaders placed great emphasis on civil government, as opposed to military, and part of this involved active sponsorship of education and scholarship. The term for the civil aspects of society, *wen* denoted the patterns of art and social refinement of the past, and the goal of perfecting "*wen* society" was not pictured in economic terms, it expressed the ambition to create a cultural flourishing that would reflect the essence of sage wisdom, as that was portrayed in the Confucian canonical texts.

In pursuit of this goal, the imperial court commissioned massive compilations of literary compendia, encyclopedias, and histories, that could bring together the now thousand-year-old traditions of the "Confucian" state. Scholarship – pure scholarship – enjoyed a prestige beyond anything seen in past eras. The government's interest in recruiting scholar-officials through the exam system became increasingly focused on the credentials of scholarship, an ideal that naturally now incorporated the artistic elements of poetry and, increasingly, calligraphy and painting, that had become central to the profile of the *literatus*.

Professor Robert Eno, Indiana University, 1990

1. According to the author, which of the following best describes the methods used by Song rulers?
    (A) The methods used by the Song were far removed from the previous ways of Chinese governments.
    (B) The Song government was organized using a degree of time-honored methods that venerated tradition.
    (C) The Song government was identical to governments of earlier Chinese dynasties.
    (D) The early Song government was influenced by the need to protect Chinese borders from nomadic invasions.

2. What was the cultural effect of the historical developments of the Song era?
    (A) The influence of Buddhism declined in most parts of China.
    (B) Chinese literacy grew as Confucianism shaped the lives of the peasant class.
    (C) Chinese cultural traditions continued and influenced neighboring regions.
    (D) The Confucian-based civil service exam was no longer a prerequisite for promotion.

3. Which of the following factors contributed most to future changes in Song political power?
    (A) increased contact with the Japanese feudal state
    (B) epidemic disease leading to the decimation of the Chinese population
    (C) military conquest of much of Central Asia including Tibet
    (D) military weakness and increasing nomadic incursions into northern China

Questions 4-6 refer to the image below.

The image above is an illustration depicting a library in Baghdad, featured in the book The Assemblies, *13th century.*

4. What can a historian surmise using the illustration?
    (A) All Muslims could read and write so that they were able to study the Quran.
    (B) There was a shortage of animal skins in the Middle East, so books were printed on paper.
    (C) Compared to Western Europe, Baghdad was a place where intellectual thought flourished in the Middle Ages.
    (D) Very few women were literate in Muslim culture.

5. The beliefs and practices of Islam, which developed in the Arabian Peninsula, reflected which of the following?
    (A) interactions among Jews, Christians, and Zoroastrians with the local Arabian peoples
    (B) the political domination of the Semitic peoples of Southwest Asia by the local Christian population
    (C) beliefs adopted from the Vedic religions and Buddhist beliefs of South Asia
    (D) Roman cultural beliefs which relegated women through the practice of *pater familias*

6. Which of the following was NOT a reason why Muslim rule expanded to many parts of Afro–Eurasia?
    (A) military expansion
    (B) activities of merchants
    (C) missionary activities of Sufis
    (D) growth of Byzantine power

Questions 7-9 refer to the image below.

The image above depicts a street scene, painted by Song Dynasty painter Zhang Zeduan, c. 1200

7. Which of the following statements would be best supported by the image above?
    (A) China was technologically advanced.
    (B) China had a thriving urban culture.
    (C) Chinese society was relatively egalitarian.
    (D) The Chinese state was fragmented.

8. Why did the economy of China flourish during the Song dynasty?
    (A) China was isolated from the political turmoil of other regions.
    (B) Nomads from Central Asia were able to transfer knowledge from the Abbasid.
    (C) Many peasants moved out of agricultural regions into cities.
    (D) Trade networks expanded resulting in increased productive capacity.

9. Which of the following is an acceptable comparison of China and Europe in the 12th and 13th centuries?
    (A) Europe was more politically fragmented than China and was characterized by decentralized monarchies.
    (B) Europe was more urbanized than China, which remained largely an agricultural society.
    (C) Gender equality in both regions increased as women were granted new social roles.
    (D) As demand for luxury goods increased the European economy flourished while that of China stagnated.

Questions 10-12 refer to the image below.

The image above is a depiction of an Arab trading ship featured in the Maqamat, *written by Al-Hariri, an Arab poet, scholar and government official of the Seljuk Empire, in 1237.*

10. Which of the following historical developments most directly contributed to development of ships like the one illustrated above?
    (A) The spread of Portuguese and Spanish navigational technology
    (B) The invention of wind-driven ships on the Nile in Ancient Egypt
    (C) Innovations in previously existing transportation technologies
    (D) The increase in the use of slave labor on ocean-going ships

11. Networks of exchange in the Indian Ocean in the period between 1200 and 1450 developed primarily because
    (A) Mongol control of the overland Silk Roads resulted in a need for safer routes.
    (B) Muslim converts in the region needed safe passage for the pilgrimage to Mecca.
    (C) Dutch and British joint-stock companies invested in larger and more powerful fleets.
    (D) environmental knowledge of wind and ocean patterns improved.

12. What was the immediate result of the increase of trading ventures in the Indian Ocean?
    (A) The British took control of India.
    (B) Powerful new trading cities developed throughout the region.
    (C) Hinduism and Buddhism spread from India into East Africa.
    (D) The power of Islam diminished in the region.

Question 13-15 refer to the passages below.

Source 1

That you wonder at so great a slaughter of men, especially of Christians and Poles, Moravians, and Hungarians, we may seem to pass it over in silence altogether, we give you this for our answer.

Because they did not obey the word of God and the command of Genghis Khan…but took council to slay our envoy, therefore God ordered us to destroy them and gave them up into our hands. For otherwise if God had not done this, what could man do to man? …we worshipping God have destroyed the whole earth from East to West in the power of God.

                                          Excerpt of a letter from the Mongol ruler, Guyuk Khan, to Pope Innocent IV, 1243

Source 2

Girls and women ride and gallop as skillfully as men. We even saw them carrying quivers and bows, and the women can ride horses for as long as the men; they have shorter stirrups, handle horses very well, and mind all the property. The Tartar (commonly used term for Mongols) women make everything: skin clothes, shoes, leggings, and everything made of leather. They drive carts and repair them, they load camels, and are quick and vigorous in all their tasks. They all wear trousers, and some of them shoot just like men.

                                            John of Plano Carpini, a Franciscan emissary to the Mongols of Pope Innocent IV, 1247

13. Which of the following represents the view MOST likely held by Guyuk Khan in his letter to the Pope?
    (A) Christians should be welcomed into the Mongol Khanates.
    (B) The polytheistic practices of the Mongols would be complimented by the Christian beliefs.
    (C) Guyuk respects the views of the Pope and looks forward to communicating with him in the future.
    (D) God favors the Mongols as can be seen by the fact that the Mongols have conquered so much of the world.

14. Which of the following is the best interpretation of the report by the Franciscan emissary?
    (A) Mongol women were treated as property by their male counterparts.
    (B) Women played a significant role in Mongol life.
    (C) Mongol women were valued similarly to other Asian cultures.
    (D) The roles of Mongolian men and women varied greatly.

15. How did the use of horse-related technology aid in the Mongolian conquests?
    (A) The use of horse-related technology decreased the mobility of the Mongol armies.
    (B) Stirrups allowed for better stability and accuracy while utilizing the bow.
    (C) Stirrups and saddles proved to be a disadvantage to warriors in the Mongol armies.
    (D) The Mongol warriors who traveled by foot were able to master horse technology.

Questions 16-18 refer to the image and passage below.

Source 1

The image above is a European depiction of the Persian physician and polymath al-Razi, treating a patient in a hospital he helped establish in Baghdad in the 9th century. The image is featured in Receuil des Traites de Medicine (Collection of Medicine Treaties), *by Gerard of Cremona, a translator of scientific books from Arabic into Latin, c. 1250.*

Source 2

The hospital shall keep all patients, men and women, until they are completely recovered. All costs are to be borne by the hospital whether the people come from afar or near, whether they are residents or foreigners, strong or weak, low or high, rich or poor, employed or unemployed, blind or signed, physically or mentally ill, learned or illiterate. There are no conditions of consideration and payment; none is objected to or even indirectly hinted at for non-payment. The entire service is through the magnificence of God, the generous one.

Policy statement of the hospital of al-Mansur Qalawun in Cairo, Egypt, c. 1284

16. What does the image reveal about Islamic medical knowledge in the 9th century?
    (A) Doctors were highly superstitious and believed Allah was responsible for the spread of most diseases.
    (B) Physicians welcomed the knowledge of European doctors as they sought to discover the origin of infectious diseases.
    (C) Doctors were well in advance of their feudal counterparts in Western Europe through their use of quarantine.
    (D) Most of Islamic medical knowledge was based on a belief in the four humors – phlegm, yellow bile, back bile, and blood.

17. The statement reveals which of the following about Islamic society in 13th-century Egypt?
    (A) There was complete equality between men and women.
    (B) The rules of behavior mirrored Muhammed's teachings in the Quran.
    (C) The only way to raise one's status in Egyptian society was through education.
    (D) Islamic society was fundamentally egalitarian with no firm hierarchy.

18. What is the best explanation of the historical context of the image of al-Razi?
    (A) Many Muslims left their homelands and migrated into France and northern Europe.
    (B) Muslim doctors were foremost in helping plague victims in the war-ravaged Balkan region.
    (C) An increase in literacy in Medieval Europe resulted in an increased interest in Islamic knowledge.
    (D) As interactions increased due to the Crusades, scientific and technological innovations spread.

Questions 19-22 refer to the image below.

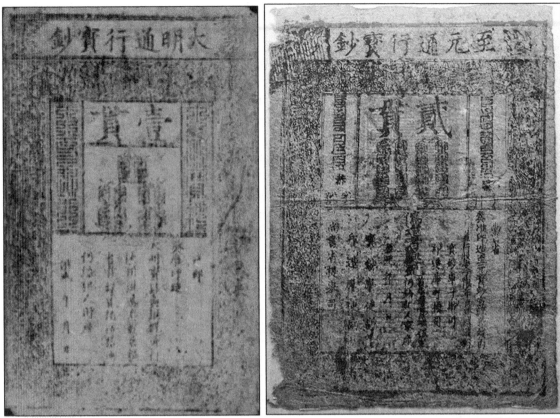

Left image: Currency from the Bureau of Paper Currency in Kaifeng, northern China, c. 1200. *Right image:* Currency from the Yuan Dynasty c. 1260.

19. Which of the following explains the most likely purpose for the creation of the currency pictured?
    (A) Expanding trade created a need for more methods of payment.
    (B) Paper currency made theft less likely on the unsafe trade routes.
    (C) Paper itself was a highly valued trade good.
    (D) Political instability made people hide their gold and silver supplies.

20. During this time period, what method of payment had been introduced by the Abbasid?
    (A) Barter
    (B) Double-entry accounting
    (C) Checking
    (D) Standardized coin weights

21. Marco Polo described paper currency in his account of China, this is an example of
    (A) The transfer of technology and innovation along trade networks.
    (B) The cultural diffusion of belief systems by merchants.
    (C) The political use of bureaucracy and spying.
    (D) The long-distance trade of luxury goods.

22. Which of the following might a modern historian conclude after studying the two artifacts?
    (A) Chinese printing techniques were quite primitive compared to European printing at the time.
    (B) Mongol rulers in China attempted to continue earlier practices that had been successful.
    (C) Paper currency was easy to forge, causing problems in the economy.
    (D) Buddhist merchants were more successful in China than were Confucian merchants.

Questions 23-26 refer to the passages below.

Source 1

We stayed one night in this island [Mombasa], and then pursued our journey to Kulwa, which is a large town on the coast. The majority of its inhabitants are Zanj, jet-black in color, and with tattoo marks on their faces. I was told by a merchant that the town of Sufala lies a fortnight's journey from Kulwa and that gold dust is brought to Sufala from Yufi in the country of the Limis, which is a month's journey distant from it. Kulwa is a very fine and substantially built town, and all its buildings are of wood. ...The sultan at the time of my visit was Abu'l-Muzaffar Hasan, who was noted for his gifts and generosity. He used to devote the fifth part of the [riches] made on his expeditions to pious and charitable purposes, as is prescribed in the Koran, and I have seen him give the clothes off his back to a mendicant who asked him for them.

        Ibn Battuta, Muslim qadi and traveler, *Travels in Asia and Africa*, c. 1340

Source 2

The women of the city maintain the custom of veiling their faces, except for the slaves who sell all the foodstuffs. The inhabitants are very rich, especially the strangers who have settled in the country; so much so that the current king has given two of his daughters in marriage to two brothers, both businessmen, on account of their wealth. There are many wells containing sweet water in Timbuktu; and in addition, when the Niger is in flood canals deliver the water to the city. Grain and animals are abundant, so that the consumption of milk and butter is considerable. But salt is in very short supply because it is carried here from Tegaza, some 500 miles from Timbuktu. I happened to be in this city at a time when a load of salt sold for eighty ducats. The king has a rich treasure of coins and gold ingots. One of these ingots weighs 970 pounds.

        Leo Africanus, Muslim diplomat, "Description of Timbuktu" from *The Description of Africa*, 1526

23. What can a historian understand about the political situation in East Africa by examining the first report?
    (A) The coastal area has been infiltrated by European powers during the "Scramble for Africa."
    (B) There is a peaceful coexistence between the Muslim interlopers and the local Zanj.
    (C) The Muslims and the Zanj are in a period of extended warfare.
    (D) The Muslims and the local Africans have formed a political alliance for mutual protection.

24. What can a historian understand about the social characteristics of Timbuktu by examining the second report?
    (A) Women in Timbuktu have few rights in marriage as they are considered socially inferior.
    (B) Merchants are considered as being less important in the social hierarchy than farmers.
    (C) The rights of elite women are restricted by male family members.
    (D) Merchants have a higher position in the social ladder than religious leaders.

25. What explains the presence of Muslim traders in both the Niger region and along the Swahili Coast?
   (A) They are there to sell luxury goods like spices and silks to African tribes.
   (B) They desire exotic African products like ivory from elephant tusks and semi-precious stones.
   (C) They plan to set up production of textiles in African centers where the labor is cheap.
   (D) They intend to profit from the precious mineral wealth of Africa.

26. Which of the following statements best compares the cultural impact of Islam in Africa with that of Christianity in the Spanish Americas between 1300 and 1600?
   (A) The Muslims used violence to impose Islam in Africa, while in the Americas the natives readily converted to Christianity.
   (B) Many Africans chose to convert to Islam for socio-economic reasons, while Americans were often pressured into taking up Christianity.
   (C) There was very little cultural impact of Islam in Africa whereas Christianity became the only religion of the Spanish viceroyalties.
   (D) The cultural impact of Islam in Africa led to restrictions on women's rights, whereas under Christianity in Spanish America women were considered equal.

Questions 27-29 refer to the image below.

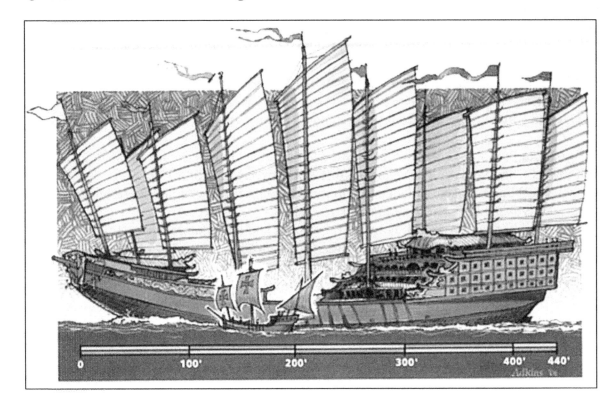

The image above depicts Zheng He's four-hundred-foot treasure ship built in the 14th century compared to Christopher Columbus' eighty-five-foot ship, the St. Maria, built a century later. Illustration by Jan Adkins, 1993.

27. What conclusion can be reached by using the illustration?
    (A) There were more forests in East Asia than in Western Europe in the 15th century.
    (B) The Ming dynasty was in need of foreign goods more than the government of Spain.
    (C) The Ming Admiral Zheng He was richer than Christopher Columbus.
    (D) The technological developments of Europe lagged behind those of China.

28. Which of the following is the most accurate description of the voyages of Zheng He?
    (A) The voyages resulted in the discovery of a sea route around the Cape of Good Hope.
    (B) The gigantic expeditions all ended in failure as little was achieved.
    (C) Zheng He made voyages in an attempt to spread the prestige of the Ming Empire.
    (D) The voyages ended when Zheng He was defeated in a naval battle by the Portuguese.

29. Which of the following was a motive for Zheng He's voyages?
    (A) The Ming had a desire to find a new route to the Americas.
    (B) The Ming wanted to thwart European naval power.
    (C) The Ming desired a way to gain tribute from neighboring countries.
    (D) The Ming sought to control Indian Ocean trade.

Questions 30-32 refer to the passage below.

I left Tangier, my birthplace, on Thursday, 2nd Rajab 725 [June 14, 1325], being at that time twenty-two years of age, with the intention of making the Pilgrimage to the Holy House and the Tomb of the Prophet… On leaving Zayla we sailed for fifteen days and came to Mogadishu, which is an enormous town. Its inhabitants are merchants and have many camels, of which they slaughter hundreds every day [for food]. When a vessel reaches the port, it is met by sumbuqs, which are small boats. …We came to Mombasa], a large island two days' journey by sea from the Swahili country. It possesses no territory on the mainland. They have fruit trees on the island, but no cereals, which have to be brought to them from the Swahil. Their food consists chiefly of bananas and fish. The inhabitants are pious, honorable, and upright, and they have well-built wooden mosques.

Ibn Battuta, Muslim qadi and traveler, excerpt from *The Rihla*, c. 1340

30. According to the excerpt, why does Ibn Battuta leave Tangier at a young age?
    (A) He was hoping to make his fortune along the lucrative Silk Road.
    (B) He was travelling as an emissary of the king of Morocco on a diplomatic mission.
    (C) He was a devout Muslim who needed to fulfil the requirements of his religious tradition.
    (D) He was looking for trading opportunities in Africa.

31. What can be surmised after reading the excerpts concerning East Africa?
    (A) The Swahili Coast was a backwater compared to the magnificence of Arabia.
    (B) There was a large export of meat and fruit from the Swahili Coast to surrounding regions.
    (C) Towns like Mombasa served as entrepots between African and Indian Ocean trade.
    (D) The Swahili Coast was isolated from Eurasia and was considered uncivilized by many.

32. How is the experience of Ibn Battuta like that of Marco Polo and Zheng He?
    (A) They all were searching for a new route to the Far East.
    (B) They were all religiously motivated with an aim of proselytizing their faith.
    (C) They were sent as spies for their respective governments.
    (D) They all wrote extensively about their travels.

Questions 33-35 refer to the following passage

The year of our blessed Savior's incarnation, 1348, that memorable mortality happened in the excellent City [Florence], far beyond all the rest in Italy; which plague, by operation of the superior bodies, or rather for our enormous iniquities, by the just anger of God was sent upon us mortals. Some few years before, it took beginning in the Eastern parts, sweeping thence an innumerable quantity of living souls: extending itself afterward from place to place Westward, until it seized on the said City. Where neither human skill or providence, could use any prevention, notwithstanding it was cleansed of many annoyances, by diligent Officers thereto deputed: besides prohibition of all sickly persons entrance, and all possible provision daily used for conservation of such as were in health, with incessant prayers and supplications of devout people for the assuaging of so dangerous a sickness.

About the beginning of the year, it also began in very strange manner…yet not as it had done in the East Countries, where Lord or Lady being touched therewith, manifest signs of inevitable death followed thereon, by bleeding at the nose. But here it began with young children, male and female, either under the armpits, or in the groin by certain swellings, in some to the bigness of an apple, in others like an egg…. In very short time after, those two infected parts were grown mortiferous [deadly], and would disperse abroad indifferently, to all parts of the body; whereupon, such was the quality of the disease, to show itself by black or blue spots, which would appear on the arms of many, others on their thighs, and every part else of the body: in some great and few, in others small and thick.

Boccaccio Giovanni, Italian author, from the introduction to *The Decameron*, 1350

33. According to Boccaccio, why did the plague arrive in Florence in the mid-14th century?
    (A) There was a very poor understanding of how diseases were transmitted in the 14th century.
    (B) Italy was isolated from most of Europe and the population had not developed an immunity to many diseases.
    (C) The city was being punished by God because of the many sins that had been committed.
    (D) Following frequent voyages of discovery, the plague was commonly transmitted from the Americas.

34. What was the probable reason for the level of trade that resulted in the arrival of the plague in the city of Florence?
    (A) The Silk Roads had flourished which promoted the growth of powerful new trading cities like Florence.
    (B) The commercial growth of Florence was facilitated by state practices and a government road system.
    (C) Trading organizations, such as the Hanseatic League resulted in Florence becoming the center of the Italian woolen region.
    (D) The expansion of the Italian Empire facilitated Afro–Eurasian trade and communication which resulted in the growth of the city.

35. What was the most important long-term impact on Western Europe of the plague pandemic of the mid-14th century?
    (A) The Italian city states witnessed a new birth of art and knowledge.
    (B) The feudal system collapsed as there were insufficient laborers in rural regions.
    (C) The power of the Catholic Church increased as survivors looked for salvation.
    (D) Women discovered increased opportunities for employment in agriculture and craft making.

Questions 36-39 refer to the passage below.

Whereas, Most Christian, High, Excellent, and Powerful Princes, King and Queen of Spain and of the Islands of the Sea, our Sovereigns, this present year 1492, after your Highnesses had terminated the war with the Moors reigning in Europe… Your Highnesses, as Catholic Christians, and princes who love and promote the holy Christian faith, and are enemies of the doctrine of [Mohammad], and of all idolatry and heresy, determined to send me, Christopher Columbus, to India, to see the princes, people, and territories, and to learn their disposition and the proper method of converting them to our holy faith; and furthermore directed that I should not proceed by land to the East, as is customary, but by a Westerly route, in which direction we have hitherto no certain evidence that any one has gone.

So after having expelled the Jews from your dominions, your Highnesses…ordered me to proceed with a sufficient armament to the regions of India, and for that purpose granted me great favors, and ennobled me that thenceforth I might call myself Don, and be High Admiral of the Sea, and perpetual Viceroy and Governor in all the islands and continents which I might discover and acquire… Hereupon I left the city of Granada, on Saturday, the twelfth day of May, 1492, and proceeded to Palos, a seaport, where I armed three vessels, very fit for such an enterprise, and having provided myself with abundance of stores and seamen, I set sail … and steered for the Canary Islands of your Highnesses which are in the said ocean, thence to take my departure and proceed till I arrived at the Indies, and perform the embassy of your Highnesses to the Princes there, and discharge the orders given me.

Christopher Columbus, in an extract from his journal written after his voyages, 1492

36. After studying the extract, what could a historian infer about Spanish cultural conditions in the late 15th century?
    (A) There was a great degree of religious toleration in Spain due to the mixture of races that lived on the Iberian Peninsula.
    (B) Many Jews lived in Spain despite the brutal policies carried out by the Spanish Inquisition.
    (C) The Spanish regarded Jews and Muslims as a threat and were determined to make Spain purely Christian.
    (D) The Spanish felt the needed to form a cultural union with India in order to guard against attacks on the Catholic Church.

37. According to the first paragraph, what motivates Columbus to set out on his initial voyage?
    (A) competition with other maritime powers
    (B) the need to earn his commission from the king and queen of Spain
    (C) the desire to proselytize Christianity to the pagan Indians
    (D) the belief that a new continent awaits his discovery

38. Which of the following best describes the short-term consequence of the voyages Columbus in the late 15th century?
- (A) The Spanish developed complex maritime technology and navigational skills that led to increased exploration.
- (B) Spanish sponsorship of Columbus dramatically increased European interest in transoceanic travel and trade.
- (C) The Spanish crown financed multiple Northern Atlantic crossings for the purpose of fishing and settlement.
- (D) American foods became staple crops in various parts of Europe, Asia, and Africa.

39. Why is the historical importance of Columbus a matter for debate amongst historians and scholars?
- (A) Many historians dispute the evidence that Columbus landed on Hispaniola as the navigation that he used was flawed.
- (B) The Vikings landed on Caribbean islands centuries before Columbus thus negating his importance.
- (C) Columbus did not actually make the voyages, and his journal was a forgery by an Italian writer who had listened to his stories in prison.
- (D) The voyages caused significant negative economic, cultural, social, and demographic changes to the native American peoples.

Questions 40-41 refer to the image below.

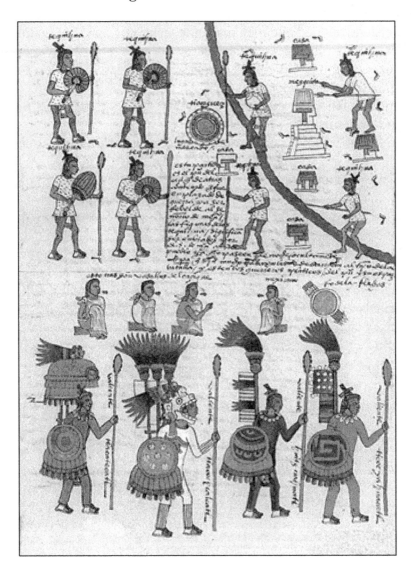

The image above is an illustration from the Codex Mendoza, *an Aztec codex, created about twenty years after the Spanish conquest of Mexico, 1542*

40. Which of the following assertions can be proven using the image from the *Codex Mendoza?*
    (A) Cultural diffusion can be seen through the use of the Latin alphabet.
    (B) Christianity was replacing traditional beliefs among the native population.
    (C) Disease had killed a large portion of the Aztec people.
    (D) The natives were adopting technology from the Europeans.

41. A modern historian might make which of the following claims after examining the image?
    (A) Aztec society was essentially egalitarian in nature.
    (B) The culture of the Aztec was relatively primitive compared to that of the Spanish.
    (C) Aztec women played no role in Aztec public life.
    (D) The Aztec society was diverse and highly organized.

Questions 42-44 refer to the passage below.

Here are many shops of artificers, and merchants, and especially of such as weave linen and cotton cloth. And hither do the Barbary [North African] merchants bring cloth of Europe. All the women of the region except maidservants go with their faces covered and sell all necessary victuals. The inhabitants, and especially strangers there residing, are exceeding rich, insomuch that the king that now is, married both his daughters unto two rich merchants. Here are many wells, containing most sweet water; and so often as the river Niger overflows, they convey the water thereof by certain sluices into the town. Corn [sorghum], cattle, milk, and butter this region yields in great abundance: but salt is very scarce here, for it is brought hither by land from Taghaza, which is five hundred miles distant. When I myself was here, I saw one camel load of salt sold for 80 ducats. The rich king of Timbuktu has many plates and scepters of gold, some of which weigh 1300 pounds; ... He has always three thousand horsemen, and a great number of footmen that shoot poisoned arrows, attending upon him. ... Here are great store of doctors, judges, priests, and other learned men, that are bountifully maintained at the king's cost and charges. And hither are brought diverse manuscripts or written books out of Barbary, which are sold for more money than any other merchandise.

Leo Africanus, an Arab traveler, from an account of the kingdom of Songhay, early 16th century

42. According to the source, which of the following is the best description of Songhay in the 16th century?
   (A) The capital, Timbuktu, was an isolated city that was restricted by environmental factors.
   (B) The kingdom flourished because of a strong economy and trade networks.
   (C) The economy of Songhay relied primarily on textile manufacturing.
   (D) The kingdom was at peace due to its remote location and cultural uniformity.

43. Which of the following was the most significant result of an increased volume of trade throughout the trans-Saharan trade network?
   (A) Gender structures changed in Sub-Saharan Africa.
   (B) Environmental processes increased with the growing demand for African goods.
   (C) Sub-Saharan African goods were integrated into the existing Eurasian trade networks.
   (D) Diasporic communities of West African merchants increased in Europe and North Africa.

44. What was the most important change in West African trade that occurred in the 16th century?
   (A) Portuguese exploration led to increased trade with West Africa as trading posts were established along the coast.
   (B) European merchants competed in transporting goods from one African market to another.
   (C) Mercantilist policies and practices were used by African rulers to expand and control their economies.
   (D) African foods became staple crops in various parts of Europe, Asia, and the Americas.

Questions 45-46 refer to the image below.

The image above depicts the court of Safavid ruler, Shah Abbas, c. 1600.

45. The panting can best be used as evidence of which of the following?
    (A) the patriarchal nature of Safavid society
    (B) the military might of the Safavids
    (C) inequalities in the Safavid social structure
    (D) the use of art to legitimize rule

46. The Safavid's greatest rivals were the Ottomans. Which of the following best explains this rivalry?
    (A) Safavid society was socially restrictive and did not like the Ottoman policies of toleration.
    (B) The Safavid were of Mongol descent and wanted to conquer their Ottoman rivals.
    (C) The Safavid were Shiite Muslims and had a long-standing feud with Sunni Muslim Ottomans.
    (D) The Safavid were an economically disadvantaged society and wanted the wealth of the Ottoman Empire.

Questions 47-49 refer to the passages below.

This country is so thoroughly covered by an intersecting network of rivers and canals that it is possible to travel almost anywhere by water. Hence, an almost incredible number of boats of every variety pass hither and thither. Indeed there are so many of them that one of the writers of our day does not hesitate to affirm that there are as many people living on the water as there are dwellers on land….

There is a certain bush from the leaves of which is decocted that celebrated drink, known to the Chinese, the Japanese, and to their neighbors as tea. … they gather its leaves in the springtime and place them in a shady place to dry, and from the dried leaves they brew a drink which they use at meals and which is served to friends when they come to visit….This beverage is sipped rather than drunk and it is always taken hot. It is not unpleasant to the taste, being somewhat bitter, and it is usually considered to be wholesome even if taken frequently. . .

From the journal of Matteo Ricci, an Italian Jesuit missionary who lived in China during the Ming Dynasty, 16th century

47. Why was China so interconnected by internal transport routes by the time Matteo Ricci visited?
    (A) Military transportation links along rivers and canals were necessary in a period of frequent interregional disputes.
    (B) Commercial growth was fostered by state-sponsored infrastructures, such as the Grand Canal.
    (C) The canals had been built by rich groups of merchants in order to carry silk and other luxury items to Chang'an, the eastern departure point of the Silk Road.
    (D) Travel by river or canal was considered safer than travel by road, which was plagued by frequent banditry.

48. Why was tea drinking confined to China and its neighbors in the 16th century?
    (A) The taste was considered too bitter by Europeans who favored beer.
    (B) China was the only region where the climatic and soil conditions were suited to growing tea.
    (C) The Chinese government made a concerted effort to control the growth and trade of tea.
    (D) Medieval doctors in Europe considered the imbibing of hot fluids to be harmful to health.

49. Why were Jesuit missionaries like Matteo Ricci sent to China in the 16th century?
    (A) They were part of a movement that aimed to create new syncretic belief systems in Asia.
    (B) They were a scholarly religious Christian group that aimed to spread and reform the Catholic church.
    (C) They were carrying out a mission to increase trade between Italian city states and East Asia during the Renaissance.
    (D) They were part of a seasoned military who were supposed to accept orders to go anywhere in the world.

Questions 50-53 refer to the passages below.

Source 1

His majesty pays much attention to various stuffs; hence Irani, European, and Mongolian articles of wear are in much abundance…. The imperial workshops in the towns of Lahore, Agra, Fatehpur, Ahmedabad and Gujarat turn out many masterpieces of workmanship, and the figures and patterns, knots and variety of fashions which now prevail astonish experienced travelers…. [A] taste for fine material has since become general, and the drapery used at feasts surpasses every description.

    Abu al- Fazl ibn Mubarak, vizier of Mughal emperor Akbar, from *Ain-i Akbari,* a logbook of the emperor's reign, c. 1600

Source 2

Large halls are seen in many places, called *karkanahs*, or workshops for the artisans. In one hall, embroiderers are busily employed, superintended by a master. Manufactures of silk, fine brocade, and other fine muslins, of which are made turbans, girdles of gold flowers, and drawers worn by females, so delicately fine as to wear out in one night might cost up to 10 or 12 crowns, or even more when embroidered with fine needlework. In this quiet and regular manner, their time glides away, no one aspiring to any improvement in the condition of life wherein he happens to have been born. The embroiderer brings up his son as an embroiderer.

    François Bernier, French physician in Mughal emperor Aurangzeb's court, *Travels in the Mughal Empire*, 1665

50. What does the first source reveal about economic developments in Eurasia in the 1450 to 1750 period?
    (A) Existing regional patterns of trade had intensified bringing prosperity and economic growth to India.
    (B) The workshops of India were independent of government control leading to individual growth but state impoverishment.
    (C) The sea routes of the Indian Ocean were central to India's textile manufacturing.
    (D) The Indian textile producers were reliant on raw materials from East Asia.

51. Akbar is considered one of the greatest rulers of the Mughal dynasty. His answer to the religious diversity and tension of India was
    (A) to promote Christianity in return for the Europeans supplying him with advanced weapons.
    (B) to attempt to crush all Hindu resistance.
    (C) to create a syncretic religion called the "divine faith" that would circumvent traditional religious rivalries.
    (D) to convert to Sikhism in order to bring peace to the subcontinent.

52. What does the second source reveal about the economy of the Mughal Empire?
    (A) Mughal economic growth depended on new forms of manufacturing and new commercial patterns.
    (B) Most of India's wealth was concentrated in the southern part of the subcontinent.
    (C) Trade was concentrated in the northern part of India allowing merchants to utilize the monsoons.
    (D) The manufacture of luxury goods made Mughal India a hub of trade.

53. What could a historian interpret from the second source concerning the social structure of India in the 17th century?
    (A) Women were considered inferior to men and were not employed in the formal economy.
    (B) The rigid caste system mandated social standing.
    (C) Workers lived with their extended families to maximize their labor potential.
    (D) The importance of textile production resulted in a growing entrepreneurial middle class.

Questions 54-55 refer to the passage below.

Mahomet Son of Emperors, Son to the famous and glorious God, Emperor of the Turks, we Command you to inform the Emperor Leopold

You have for some time past acted to our prejudice, and violated our Friendship, although we have not offended you, neither by War, or any otherwise; but you have taken private advice with other Kings, and your Councils how to take off your Yoke, in which you have acted very Indiscreetly, and thereby have exposed your People to fear and danger, having nothing to expect but Death, which you have brought upon your selves. For I declare unto you, I will make myself your Master, pursue you from East to West, and extend my Majesty to the end of the Earth; in all which you shall find my Power to your great prejudice. I assure you that you shall feel the weight of my Power; and for that you have put your hope and expectation in the strength of some Towns and Castles, I have given command to overthrow them, and to trample under feet with my Horses, all that is acceptable and pleasant in your Eyes, leaving nothing hereafter by which you shall make a friendship with me, or any fortified places to put your trust in: For I have resolved without retarding of time, to ruin both you and your People, to take the German Empire according to my pleasure, and to leave in the Empire a Commemoration of my dreadful Sword, that it may appear to all, it will be a pleasure to me, to give a public establishment of my Religion, and to pursue your Crucified God, ... You will therefore do well to forsake your Religion, or else I will give Order to Consume you with Fire. This is enough said unto you, and to give you to understand what I would have, in case you have a mind to know it.

The Great Turks Declaration of War against the Emperor of Germany, 1683

54. What seems to be the most important goal of the war against Leopold?
    (A) to expand the Ottoman Empire
    (B) to ruin the economic power of Germany
    (C) to enslave the Germans as part of the *devshirme*
    (D) to form a trade agreement with the Germans

55. Which of the following explains why the Turks may have been willing to go to war with the Germans at this point in history?
    (A) The Turks had gunpowder technology while their neighbors still did not.
    (B) Religious turmoil in Europe had weakened most of the Christian kingdoms.
    (C) Diseases, like the Black Death, had destroyed European armies.
    (D) The Silk Road was failing, and the Turks were in need of new trade routes.

MC Test 2: 1200 to 2001

Questions 1-3 refer to the passage below.

The Great Khan resides in the capital city of Cathay which is called Cambaluc. It is enclosed all round by a great wall forming a square, each side of which is a mile in length. It is also very thick, and a good ten paces in height, whitewashed and loop-holed all round. At each angle of the wall there is a very fine and rich palace in which the war-harness of the Emperor is kept, such as bows and arrows, saddles and bridles, and bowstrings, and everything necessary for an army. Also midway between every two of these corner palaces there is another of the like' so that in the whole enclosure you find eight vast palaces stored with the Great Lord's harness of war.

The Emperor's Mint then is in this same City of Cambaluc, and …he makes his money after this fashion. He makes them take of the bark of a certain tree, in fact of the Mulberry Tree, the leaves of which are the food of the silkworms—these trees being so numerous that whole districts are full of them. What they take is a certain fine white skin which lies between the wood of the tree and the thick outer bark, and this they make into something resembling sheets of paper, but black….There is a kind worth one Bezant of gold, and others of three Bezants, and so up to ten. All these pieces of paper are [issued with as much solemnity and authority as if they were of pure gold or silver; and on every piece a variety of officials, whose duty it is, have to write their names, and to put their seals. And when all is prepared duly, the chief officer deputed by the Khan smears the Seal entrusted to him with vermilion, and impresses it on the paper, so that the form of the Seal remains printed upon it in red; the money is then authentic.

Excerpt from The Travels of Marco Polo, late 13th century

1. To what is Marco Polo referring to in the second paragraph of the excerpt?
   (A) the cultivation of mulberry trees, sericulture and silk-making
   (B) the printing of books using wooden blocks
   (C) the necessary ingredients for a strong paper currency
   (D) the practice of alchemy in the Mongol pursuit of wealth

2. A historian would most likely use the first paragraph of the excerpt to prove which of the following?
   (A) Marco Polo was an important figure in Venetian and Chinese history.
   (B) The culture of the Yuan dynasty was influenced by its roots in nomadic warfare of the Central Asian steppes.
   (C) Cambaluc was much bigger than other Chinese cities at this time.
   (D) Many scholars during the Mongolian Yuan dynasty had a Confucian education.

3. According to the second paragraph of the excerpt, which of the following statements can be asserted?
   (A) The economy of China under the Yuan dynasty was centered on trade along the Silk Roads.
   (B) The Chinese economy was mainly dominated by free enterprise with little government involvement in this period.
   (C) Trade was flourishing in China and there was a need to supplement metal coinage with paper money.
   (D) Marco Polo was intimately aware of the economic affairs of Kublai Khan.

Questions 4-6 refer to the passage below.

I made my way to Cathay, the realm of the Emperor of the Tartars [Mongols] who is called the Grand Khan. To him I presented the letter of our lord the Pope and invited him to adopt the Catholic Faith of our Lord Jesus Christ, but he had grown too old in idolatry. However, he bestows many kindnesses upon the Christians, and these two years past I am abiding with him…

I have built a church in the city of Cambaluc (Beijing), in which the king has his chief residence. … I have baptized there, as well as I can estimate, up to this time some 6000 persons…and I am often still engaged in baptizing.

Also, I have gradually bought one hundred and fifty boys, the children of pagan parents, and of ages varying from seven to eleven, who had never learned any religion. These boys I have baptized, and I have taught them Greek and Latin after our manner.

As for the road hither, I may tell you that the way through the land of the Goths, subject to the Emperor of the Northern Tartars, is the shortest and safest; and by it the friars might come, along with the letter-carriers, in five or six months. The other route again is very long and very dangerous, involving two sea-voyages….

John of Monte Corvino, a Franciscan priest, from a report to Rome, 1305

4. What is the most likely purpose of the report?
   (A) The priest wants the pope to send more priests as he has so many heathens to convert.
   (B) The priest feels the need to let his superiors know that he has successfully converted many Mongols.
   (C) The priest sees the opportunity of converting the Grand Khan to Christianity if he has support from Rome.
   (D) The priest wants to warn other Christians about the dangers of travelling across the Asian steppes.

5. What historical process contributed to the type of interaction illustrated in the report?
   (A) Increased warfare in Eurasia resulted in the cultural isolation of much of Asia.
   (B) The construction of trading centers increased the wealth and influence of merchants.
   (C) Interregional contacts between states encouraged cultural transfers.
   (D) The European Reformation resulted in an increase in proselytizing Christianity.

6. What was an important consequence of the Mongol domination of much of Eurasia?
   (A) Eurasian trade and communication increased as the Mongol Empire grew.
   (B) The Mongol religion spread into many regions including Russia.
   (C) Most Mongols eventually settled in urban areas and became involved in commerce.
   (D) Many Eurasian states formed alliances to combat the danger of Mongol invasion.

Questions 7-9 refer to the image below.

The image above depicts a page from The Book of Hours, *a popular Christian devotional book from France, c. 1410.*

7. What can historians learn from the illustration about agriculture in Western Europe in the Middle Ages?
   (A) Wheat was the principle staple crop in this period.
   (B) The fields of medieval farms were left fallow for most of the year.
   (C) Technological innovations like the horse collar were introduced to increase production.
   (D) The agricultural workers were houses in small cottages on the fringe of large holdings.

8. What role did castles like the one in the image play in the social and political life of people of Western Europe between 1200 and 1450?
   (A) They were constructed to illustrate the power of the lords compared to that of the church.
   (B) They were the center of commercial activities such as fairs and markets.
   (C) They were used as a place of refuge by the peasants when danger threatened.
   (D) They were made to attract rich visitors to the region.

9. What form of labor was most common in Western Europe in the period 1200 to 1450?
   (A) slavery in iron and tin mines
   (B) serfdom in rural areas
   (C) plantation labor in commercial farms
   (D) debt slavery in urban areas

Questions 10-13 refer to the image below.

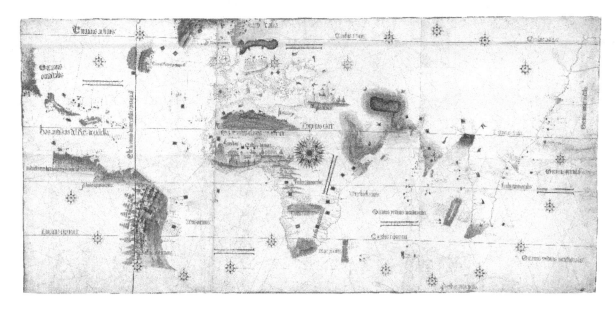

The image above depicts the Cantino Planisphere, *made in Portugal in 1502. It is the oldest surviving map of the known world at the time of European exploratory voyages.*

10. The map above would be most useful in examining which of the following?
    (A) Ferdinand Magellan's circumnavigation of the globe
    (B) the arrival of the Portuguese in the Japanese port of Tanegashima
    (C) the explorations of Christopher Columbus to the Caribbean
    (D) the seven voyages of Zheng He

11. The *Cantino Planisphere* is the earliest existing nautical chart where places are depicted according to their astronomically observed latitudes. Which of the following made this possible?
    (A) the use of Marco Polo's journal to accurately measure the distance from Italy to China
    (B) the mariner's astrolabe reintroduced into Europe by Arabs
    (C) the celestial observations of Galileo and his calculations of the movements of the planets
    (D) the magnetic compass first used by the Venetians in the late 13th century

12. In 1498, shortly before the map was produced, Vasco da Gama voyaged to coastal India; this voyage resulted in which of the following?
    (A) the political domination of India by the Portuguese
    (B) the weakening of Muslim control of trade from Asia
    (C) a decrease in the desire for Asian goods in Europe
    (D) the immediate economic decline of the Ming Dynasty

13. The most prevalent reason for 15th and 16th century voyages of exploration was…
    (A) to achieve personal enrichment.
    (B) to discover barbarian peoples.
    (C) to gain direct access to goods from Asia.
    (D) to proselytize the Christian faith.

Questions 14-15 refer to the image and passage below.

Source 1

The image above is an illustration of a tomato plant by Italian physician and botanist, Pietro Andrea, called Poma Aurea [Golden Apple], *1544.*

Source 2

No matter how you prepare it [the potato], the root is tasteless and starchy. It cannot be regarded as an enjoyable food, but it provides abundant, reasonably healthy food for men who want nothing but sustenance.

Diderot, French philosopher, from his Encyclopedia, c. 1755

14. Which of the following historical developments best explains the background to the two sources?
    (A) New connections between the Eastern and Western Hemispheres resulted in the Columbian Exchange.
    (B) Following Portuguese exploration, African crops were brought to Europe and became popular.
    (C) Repeated bad harvests of European crops resulted in the need to find alternative foods for a growing population.
    (D) The Italian and French middle class used their wealth to acquire foreign luxury goods.

15. What was the most important result of the world-wide spread of potatoes?
    (A) There was a general increase in food supply and famines became rare.
    (B) The staple food of both the French and the Chinese became potatoes.
    (C) Populations in Afro–Eurasia benefitted nutritionally leading to population growth.
    (D) American food crops ousted African traditional crops

Questions 16-18 refer to the passage below.

At Buda I made my first acquaintance with the Janissaries; this is the name by which the Turks call the infantry of the royal guard. The Turkish state has 12,000 of these troops when the corps is at its full strength. They are scattered through every part of the empire, either to garrison the forts against the enemy, or to protect the Christians and Jews from the violence of the mob. There is no district with any considerable amount of population, no borough or city, which has not a detachment of Janissaries to protect the Christians, Jews, and other helpless people from outrage and wrong…

In making his appointments the Sultan pays no regard to any pretensions on the score of wealth or rank, nor does he take into consideration recommendations or popularity, he considers each case on its own merits, and examines carefully into the character, ability, and disposition of the man whose promotion is in question. It is by merit that men rise in the service, a system which ensures that posts should only be assigned to the competent. Each man in Turkey carries in his own hand his ancestry and his position in life, which he may make or mar as he will. Those who receive the highest offices from the Sultan are for the most part the sons of shepherds or herdsmen, and so far from being ashamed of their parentage, they actually glory in it…. Among the Turks, therefore, honors, high posts, and judgeships are the rewards of great ability and good service. If a man be dishonest, or lazy, or careless, he remains at the bottom of the ladder, an object of contempt; for such qualities there are no honors in Turkey!"

> Ogier Ghiselin de Busbecq, Flemish ambassador of the Holy Roman Emperor to the Turkish Sultan's court in Istanbul during the reign of Süleyman the Magnificent, from *The Turkish Letters*, 1554

16. According to the ambassador's letter, which of the following descriptions of the Ottoman Empire is correct?
    (A) The Ottomans were intolerant of any religions other than Islam.
    (B) Most important positions in the Ottoman Empire were held by foreigners recruited through the *devshirme* system of Janissaries.
    (C) Women had very little political role to play apart from behind the scenes.
    (D) There was a merit-based system of advancement under the Ottomans.

17. The Janissaries were recruited through *devshirme*, which was a system…
    (A) designed to determine which women in the harem would marry and have children with the emperor.
    (B) created in order to fill positions in the military and bureaucracy with men trained from childhood.
    (C) formed with the aim of appointing both Christian and Muslim administrators in Northern India.
    (D) intended to provide a pool of translators who could ensure the laws devised in Turkish were understood by all.

18. Which of the following is another example of a method used by rulers to legitimize and consolidate their power between 1450 and 1750?
    (A) The Safavid emperors' use of human sacrifice
    (B) Chinese emperors' public performance of Christian rituals
    (C) The Mughal leaders' use of education and an exam system
    (D) European kings' construction of palaces like Versailles

Questions 19-21 refer to the passages below.

Source 1

The tsar labored at the reform of fashions, or, more properly speaking, of dress. Until that time the Russians had always worn long beards, which they cherished and preserved with much care, allowing them to hang down on their bosoms, without even cutting the moustache. With these long beards they wore the hair very short, except the ecclesiastics, who, to distinguish themselves, wore it very long. The tsar, in order to reform that custom, ordered that gentlemen, merchants, and other subjects, except priests and peasants, should each pay a tax of one hundred rubles a year if they wished to keep their beards; the commoners had to pay one kopek each…and there were many old Russians who, after having their beards shaved off, saved them preciously, in order to have them placed in their coffins, fearing that they would not be allowed to enter heaven without their beards. As for the young men, they followed the new custom with the more readiness as it made them appear more agreeable to the fair sex.

Jean Rousset de Missy, *Life of Peter the Great*, c. 1730

Source 2

He is mechanically turned, and seems designed by nature rather to be a ship carpenter than a great prince. This was his chief study and exercise while he stayed here [England]. He wrought much with his own hands and made all about him work at the models of his ships. He told me he designed a great fleet at Azov and with it to attack the Turkish Empire. But he did not seem capable of conducting so great a design, though his conduct in his wars since this has discovered a greater genius in him than appeared at this time.

Bishop Burnet, *Peter the Great,* 1698

19. According to Jean Rousset de Missy, what problem did Russia face in the early 18th century that Peter the Great was determined to rectify?
 (A) Russian society was dominated by the Orthodox Church and its adherents.
 (B) There were huge disparities between the social classes in Russia.
 (C) The perception that Russia lagged behind Western Europe in its cultural development.
 (D) Russia was faced with an aging population and poor healthcare.

20. What was a foreign problem that Peter the Great had to contend with in the late 17th century?
 (A) Russia was at war constantly throughout his reign.
 (B) There were no nations in Europe willing to make agreements with Russia.
 (C) Russia was threatened by the expansionist designs of the Qing Empire to the east.
 (D) The Ottoman Empire was a threat to Russia's southern border.

21. Russia's interactions and interests in the West at this time…
 (A) dramatically altered Russian Orthodox beliefs.
 (B) replaced agriculture with industrialism and mercantilism.
 (C) did not alter the fundamental agricultural characteristics of Russia.
 (D) had a more positive impact on the peasants than on the nobility.

Questions 22-24 refer to the passage below.

Manorial Lords and Subjects;
The servile status of subjects is herewith abolished completely and the following dispositions enacted:
• Any subject is entitled to marry, subject to previous notification and acquisition of a certificate, to be delivered free of charge.
• He may, provided he observes the regulations governing conscription for military service, leave his present manor and settle or take service on another within the Province; but if he wishes to establish himself as a peasant cultivator or cottager on another manor, he must ask for a leaving certificate, which must also be issued him free of charge, to be shown to the new manorial authority.
• A subject is free to learn any handicraft, trade, etc., and seek his livelihood where he will. For this no leaving permit is necessary.

Emperor Joseph II of Austria, *The Serfdom Patent,* 1781

22. What rights is Emperor Joseph II granting to the serfs of Austria?
    (A) He grants them equal rights to the landowning class.
    (B) He grants them the right to rise up against social abuses inherent in the system.
    (C) He grants them the rights to freedom of movement and employment.
    (D) He grants them the right to own serfs of their own.

23. Joseph was influenced by Enlightenment ideas to challenge existing notions of social relations; other "enlightened despots" were also influenced, which can be seen by…
    (A) how they adopted mercantilism.
    (B) how they granted religious toleration.
    (C) how they became involved in colonialism.
    (D) how they built monumental architecture.

24. Which other monarch of this era also considered the issue of serfdom but ultimately took no action?
    (A) George III of Britain
    (B) Louis XVI of France
    (C) Mehmet of the Ottoman Empire
    (D) Catherine II of Russia

Questions 25-27 refer to the passages below.

Source 1

What is the Third Estate? Everything.
What has it been until now in the political order? Nothing.
What does it want to be? Something.

                        Abbé Emmanuel-Joseph Sieyès, French political writer, January 1789

Source 2

We swear never to separate ourselves from the National Assembly, and to reassemble wherever circumstances require, until the constitution of the realm is drawn up and fixed upon solid foundations.
                Excerpt from an agreement signed at Versailles on June 2, 1789

25. Why did Abbé Sieyès write these words in a pamphlet that was distributed all over France?
    (A) He was attempting to gain support for King Louis XVI.
    (B) He wanted to restore the former glory of the Catholic Church after a Huguenot upsurge.
    (C) He was trying to achieve a fair distribution of power in the French political system.
    (D) He wanted to ensure that the peasants of France were not driven out of their jobs by immigrants.

26. What was the most immediate result of the agreement signed at Versailles?
    (A) Thousands were executed by guillotine because they refused to accept the rule of the National Assembly.
    (B) Angry Parisians took control of the Bastille fortress to secure weapons for the troubles ahead.
    (C) The French nation stopped believing in Catholic dogma and most of the citizens turned to atheism.
    (D) Napoleon seized control of the government, effectively ending the revolution.

27. What political change occurred in France in the time between the two passages?
    (A) King Louis XVI abdicated and France became a republic.
    (B) The guillotine was first used to silence those against the revolution.
    (C) The *Declaration of the Rights of Man and of the Citizen* was created.
    (D) The Third Estate demanded an equal vote when the Estates General met at Versailles.

Questions 28-29 refer to the image and passage below.

Source 1

The image above depicts a political cartoon drawn by British artist James Gillray, titled "A Family of Sans Culotts refreshing after the fatigues of the day," 1792.

Source 2

What was the aim of those bristling men who in . . . revolutionary chaos, ragged, howling, wild, with tomahawk raised, and pike aloft, rushed over old over-turned Paris? They desired the end of oppressions, the end of tyrannies, the end of the sword, labor for man, instruction for children, social gentleness for woman, liberty, equality, fraternity, bread for all, ideas for all.

Victor Hugo, from his novel *Les Miserables,* 1862

28. What is the BEST explanation of why Gillray created the cartoon?
    (A) He made it as the cover page to the short story, *A Modest Proposal*.
    (B) It was intended as propaganda against the French Revolution.
    (C) It was designed to show the depths that Napoleon's army sank to while invading much of Europe.
    (D) It was made to depict the extreme tortures the *Grand Blancs* used against the slaves in Haiti.

29. Which of the following is the best comparison of the two sources above?
    (A) They are both supportive of the struggle by the common people against oppression.
    (B) They differ in that the cartoon is more barbaric than the excerpt from the novel.
    (C) While both acknowledge the violence, Hugo is more supportive of the aims of the revolutionaries.
    (D) Gillray is critical of the barbarism, whereas Hugo ignores the inherent violence.

Questions 30-32 refer to the image below.

30. The cartoon was intended to most clearly illustrate which of the following?
    (A) The level of crime in 19th century London was higher in the dockland areas near the River Thames.
    (B) The refusal of the British government to take any action about the issues raised by high levels of air pollution
    (C) The need for the British government to be made aware of major social issues caused by industrialization
    (D) The increase in prostitution which was causing an increase in unwanted children

31. Urban growth led to many problems that demanded concerted government action by the late 19th century. Which of the following was a measure taken in that period?
    (A) Sewer systems were built to combat water-borne diseases.
    (B) Suburbs were built outside of cities as lower-class workers fled the city.
    (C) Deforested areas were replanted in an effort to improve air quality.
    (D) Factories were charged a carbon tax for the amount of air pollution they generated.

32. The problems caused by rapid population growth in the 19th century Europe led to which of the following?
    (A) policies of limiting the number of children per family through government regulations
    (B) increasing emigration to the Americas by Europeans looking for economic opportunities
    (C) massive famines all over Europe that led to social unrest and riots
    (D) a mass movement of workers from Western Europe to Eastern Europe in search of work

Questions 33-35 refer to the chart below.

"Length of Railways Open for Traffic, and the Various Traffic" British records, 1860

	Presidencies or Provinces	1854	1855	1856	1857	1858	1859
		Miles	Miles	Miles	Miles	Miles	Miles
Length of Line Open for Traffic	Bengal	-	121	121	121	121	142
	North-West Provinces	-	-	-	-	-	-
	Madras	-	-	-	65	81	96
	Bombay	35	35	88	85	130	194
	Sind	-	-	-	-	-	-
	Punjab	-	-	-	-	-	-
		No.	No.	No.	No.	No.	No.
Passengers Conveyed	Bengal	-	383,744	838,858	1,018,688	1,103,634	1,271,932
	North-West Provinces	-	-	-	-	-	-
	Madras	-	-	-	164,056	207,282	288,949
	Bombay	535,19	487,764	507,014	647,112	819,893	1,161,501
	Sind	-	-	-	-	-	-
	Punjab	-	-	-	-	-	-
		£	£	£	£	£	£
Receipts from Goods Traffic	Bengal	-	23,497	43,799	54,484	58,856	73,947
	North-West Provinces	-	-	-	-	-	-
	Madras	-	-	-	12,753	17,051	25,303
	Bombay	13,647	12,512	14,714	25,486	35,224	60,785
	Sind	-	-	-	-	-	-
	Punjab	-	-	-	-	-	-

33. Which of the following statements is best supported by the chart?
    (A) The population of the North West Provinces was insufficient to merit a railway system.
    (B) The British built an extensive railway system to enable more efficient interregional Indian commerce.
    (C) The population of India grew rapidly in the late 19th century.
    (D) The province of Bengal became increasingly important as an economic hub of British India.

34. What historical development was most the important reason for the growth of the Indian railway system?
    (A) The development of new technology made it possible to take advantage of new resources of energy stored in fossil fuels.
    (B) The British needed to transport large amounts of manufactured goods from its colonies to supply a growing domestic demand.
    (C) The British needed to move colonial soldiers quickly to fight in large-scale international warfare.
    (D) The economic competition among British colonies in Asia and Africa led the colonies to build more and more infrastructure.

35. What was the long-term economic result of European imperialism in the Middle East and Asia?
    (A) Western technology was diffused into these regions allowing them to compete with European industry.
    (B) While Middle Eastern and Asian countries continued to produce manufactured goods, these regions' share in global manufacturing declined.
    (C) Christianity made significant gains in some regions; however, most people maintained their traditional beliefs.
    (D) Governments in these regions became democratic, leading up to independence.

Questions 36-38 refer to the passages below.

Source 1

The future and wealth of France depend above all on the extension and prosperity of our colonies. When factories produce more than consumers need, work must stop for a time, and workers, condemned to inactivity for a more or less long period, must live off their savings and suffer without there being any possibility to institute a remedy for the evil. The reasons for the abnormal situation can be boiled down to a lack of markets for our products. Once the French genius is put to colonization we will find a draining of our overflow of our factories, and at the same time we will be able to secure, at the source of production, the primary, materials needed in our factories.

"Imperial Conquest: The Nation's Savior," *Le Petit Journal, 1883*

Source 2

We hold that the policy known as imperialism is hostile to liberty and tends toward militarism, an evil from which it has been our glory to be free. We regret that it has become necessary in the land of Washington and Lincoln to reaffirm that all men, of whatever race or color, are entitled to life, liberty, and the pursuit of happiness. We maintain that governments derive their just powers from the consent of the governed. We insist that the subjugation of any people is "criminal aggression" and open disloyalty to the distinctive principles of our government.

Platform of the American Anti-Imperialist League, 1899

36. How does the author of Source 1 justify imperialism in the late 19th century?
    (A) He claims that the French are racially superior to their colonial subjects.
    (B) He indicates that French imperialism is necessary to halt the expansion of the British Empire.
    (C) He asserts that a fully employed industrial workforce will combat the spread of communist ideas.
    (D) He uses the capitalist argument of the logic of supply and demand.

37. What does Source 2 warn will happen if imperialism in the late 19th century continues unabated?
    (A) The inevitable consequence will be a weakening of American power.
    (B) The imperialism will lead to a resurgence in slavery despite emancipation.
    (C) The result of a new wave of imperialism will threaten world peace.
    (D) The disparity between the industrialized states and the non-industrialized states will increase.

38. What is the eventual outcome of imperialism in the mid and late 20th century?
    (A) After the end of World War II, some colonies negotiated independence, while others achieved independence through armed struggle.
    (B) By the beginning of World War I, there were very few regions of Asia and Africa still colonized.
    (C) Violent decolonization struggles resulted in a decline in world population in the late 20th century.
    (D) The League of Nations were successful in quelling imperialistic uprisings and ensuring collective security.

Questions 39-41 refer to the passage below.

The whole Anglo-Egyptian army advanced westward, in a line nearly two miles long, and drove the Dervishes [Sudanese] before them into the deserts, so that they could by no means rally or re-form... Sir H. Kitchener shut up his glasses, and, remarking that he thought the enemy had been given "a good dusting," gave the order for the brigades to resume their interrupted march on Omdurman...

Meanwhile the great Dervish army, which had advanced at sunrise in hope and courage, fled in utter rout... and leaving more than 20,000 warriors dead and even greater numbers wounded behind them. [By contrast, the Anglo-Egyptian Army suffered losses of 48 dead.] Thus ended the Battle of Omdurman—the most signal triumph ever gained by science over barbarians. Within the space of five hours the strongest and best-armed savage army yet arrayed against a modern European Power had been destroyed and dispersed, with hardly any difficulty, comparatively small risk, and insignificant loss to the victors.

Winston Churchill, British military officer, 1898

39. Which of the following is the most reasonable explanation of the uneven battle described in the excerpt?
   (A) The Dervish Sudanese were vastly outnumbered by their enemies.
   (B) The climate of the region caused the soldiers to die from the heat.
   (C) The Anglo-Egyptians had superior weapon technology.
   (D) The French decided not to fight for the Sudan and withdrew their troops.

40. The Battle of Omdurman was one of many conflicts that occurred in Africa during the 19th century at a time when...
   (A) industrializing powers were establishing transoceanic empires.
   (B) most European states were using diplomacy to expand their empires in Africa.
   (C) Africans were becoming aware of their desire to form nation states.
   (D) Europe was competing with the United States for global political and economic dominance.

41. What was the main difference between African colonies like Sudan or the Congo and those like Kenya and Algeria?
   (A) Mineral wealth caused the Sudan and the Congo to be colonized to a greater extent than Kenya and Algeria.
   (B) Kenya and Algeria attracted more white settlers than Sudan and the Congo because of the climate and farming opportunities.
   (C) The colonization of Sudan and the Congo was more violent and repressive than that of Kenya and Algeria.
   (D) The Sudan and Congo were colonized because they provided a bigger market for industrial goods than Algeria or Kenya.

Questions 42-44 refer to the passages below.

Source 1

As for those regions lying within those frontiers wherein Great Britain is free to act without detriment to the interests of her ally, France, I am empowered in the name of the Government of Great Britain to give the following assurances…Great Britain is prepared to recognise and support the independence of the Arabs in all the regions within the limits demanded by the Sherif of Mecca… When the situation admits, Great Britain will give to the Arabs her advice and will assist them to establish what may appear to be the most suitable forms of government in those various territories…I am convinced that this declaration will assure you beyond all possible doubt of the sympathy of Great Britain towards the aspirations of her friends the Arabs and will result in a firm and lasting alliance, the immediate results of which will be the expulsion of the Turks from the Arab countries and the freeing of the Arab peoples from the Turkish yoke, which for so many years has pressed heavily upon them.

> Sir Henry McMahon, British High Commissioner in Egypt, excerpts from a letter to Ali ibn Husain, the Sherif of Mecca, 1915

Source 2

To those colonies and territories which as a consequence of the late war have ceased to be under the sovereignty of the States which formerly governed them and which are inhabited by peoples not yet able to stand by themselves under the strenuous conditions of the modern world, there should be applied the principle that the well-being and development of such peoples form a sacred trust of civilisation and that securities for the performance of this trust should be embodied in this Covenant.

Certain communities formerly belonging to the Turkish Empire have reached a stage of development where their existence as independent nations can be provisionally recognized subject to the rendering of administrative advice and assistance by a Mandatory until such time as they are able to stand alone. The wishes of these communities must be a principal consideration in the selection of the Mandatory.

> Article 22 of the Treaty of Versailles, signed 1919

42. In Source 1, what does the representative of the British government imply is the British pledge concerning the Arabs living in the Middle East?
    (A) The British will aid the Arabs in resisting the ambitions of the French in the region.
    (B) The British are willing to advise the Arabs in setting up government in the region previously occupied by the Ottoman Empire.
    (C) The British plan to give assistance to the Arab people of the region to create a constitutional monarchy like that of Great Britain.
    (D) The British desire to create a military alliance with the Sherif of Mecca in order to expel Ottoman forces.

43. What plan does Article 22 of the Treaty of Versailles designate for the states previously controlled by the Ottomans?
    (A) The states of the Middle East will be given full sovereignty over their own political organization.
    (B) The states who have proved themselves loyal to the British and French during World War I will be rewarded.
    (C) The states that were formerly a part of the Ottoman Empire will be administered by European advisors until they are capable of self-rule.
    (D) The Middle East will be given self-determination as advised by the U.S. president, Woodrow Wilson.

44. The former colonies of which other empire were designated to be treated like those of the Ottoman Empire?
    (A) the French Empire
    (B) the German Empire
    (C) the Japanese Empire
    (D) the Russian Empire

Questions 45-47 refer to the images below.

Left image: German poster from 1918 featuring the words "War loans help the guardians of your happiness." Right image: French poster from 1919 featuring the words "For the Flag! For Victory! Subscribe to the National Loan."

45. What message was Poster 1 designed to send to the German people?
    (A) Giving money to help the German war effort would ensure German economic growth.
    (B) Aiding the German military would safeguard the future of the German nation.
    (C) Assisting the war effort would lead to a higher birth rate in Germany.
    (D) The French were willing to go to any lengths to recover Alsace-Lorraine.

46. How did the artist of Poster 2 try to influence the French to donate to the war effort?
    (A) He used anti-German sentiment to increase the impact of the design.
    (B) He portrayed the French maiden as having been defiled by the invading Germans.
    (C) He used the passion of the French Revolution by glorifying the struggle needed to make the French Republic.
    (D) He exaggerated the poverty of France to increase the amount that the government raised for the war effort.

47. Which of the following is most similar to the production of posters like the two shown above during World War I?
    (A) The use of trench warfare on the Western Front
    (B) Cubist art in the interwar years
    (C) The cultivation of Victory Gardens
    (D) The exclusion of women and minorities

Questions 48-51 refer to the passages below.

Source 1

Peaceful surrender of power by the bourgeoisie is possible, if it is convinced that resistance is hopeless and if it prefers to save its skin. It is much more likely, of course, that even in small states socialism will not be achieved without civil war, and for that reason the only program of international Social-Democracy must be recognition of civil war, though violence is, of course, alien to our ideals.
                V.I. Lenin, *A Caricature of Marxism and Imperialist Economism*, 1916

Source 2

A revolution is not a dinner party, or writing an essay, or painting a picture, or doing embroidery; it cannot be so refined, so leisurely and gentle, so temperate, kind, courteous, restrained and magnanimous. A revolution is an insurrection, an act of violence by which one class overthrows another.
        Mao Zedong, *Report on an Investigation of the Peasant Movement in Hunan*, 1927

48. What similarity between the Russian and Chinese communist revolutions can be supported by the excerpts above?
    (A) Their leaders both believed that socialism could be achieved through non-violent means.
    (B) Their leaders believed class hierarchies were natural and unavoidable.
    (C) Their leaders encouraged the use of violence in achieving a socialist state.
    (D) Their leaders believed that socialism could be achieved through gradual legislative changes.

49. What is ANOTHER similarity between the Russian and Chinese communist revolutions?
    (A) Both revolutions were preceded by moderate nationalist revolutions.
    (B) Both revolutions sought to revive traditional gender roles.
    (C) Both revolutions sought to abolish the feudal order.
    (D) Both revolutions received substantial support from foreign countries.

50. What was one similar result of the Russian and Chinese communist revolutions?
    (A) Both economies focused on production of high-demand luxury goods.
    (B) Both economies remained unindustrialized and agrarian.
    (C) Both societies became open to foreign influence and cultural diversity.
    (D) Both governments enforced repressive policies that negatively affected their populations.

51. Which of the following statements best explains the difference between the Mexican Revolution in the early 20th century and the communist revolutions of Russia and China?
    (A) The Mexican Revolution arose in opposition to neocolonialism whereas the communist revolutions were a fight against social inequality.
    (B) The Mexican Revolution was led by religious leaders whereas the communist revolutions were led by middle class intellectuals.
    (C) The main aim of the Mexican Revolution was to overthrow the monarchy whereas the communist aim was to end economic imperialism.
    (D) The Mexican Revolution did not involve violence whereas the revolutions in China and Russia led to the death of thousands.

Questions 52-55 refer to the graph below.

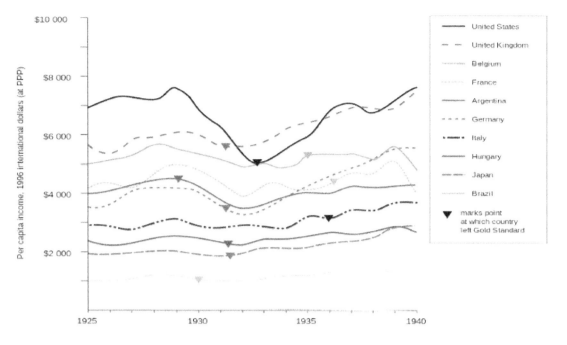

Global Great Depression

A graph depicting the per capita income of 10 nations from 1925 to 1940.

52. What does the graph indicate concerning world economic conditions in the 1920s and 1930s?
    (A) South American states were making considerable economic progress in the 1920s.
    (B) Leaving the Gold Standard had no effect on a country's economic position.
    (C) Europe was suffering an economic downturn before the United States.
    (D) The United States' economy was unaffected by developments in Europe.

53. One economic problem in the 1920's that led to the Depression was
    (A) a surplus of gold in government treasuries.
    (B) the over production and under consumption leading to falling prices.
    (C) the collapse of the cotton market in the American South.
    (D) dangerous underproduction and shortages.

54. During the Depression most nations…
    (A) practiced economic nationalism.
    (B) pushed for an expansion of trade.
    (C) cooperated on a global scale to fight the problem on a scale never seen before.
    (D) dramatically reduced tariffs in an effort to facilitate international trade.

55. The Soviet Union was less affected by the world-wide Depression. The BEST explanation for this is…
    (A) Communism was successful in strengthening the Soviet economy by 1923.
    (B) the Soviets were relatively uninvolved in global trade.
    (C) the Soviets were not industrialized as the 5 Year Plans all failed.
    (D) the Soviets strengthened their economy by concentrating on militarization under Lenin.

Multiple-Choice Questions

MC Test 3: 1200 to 2001

Questions 1-3 refer to the passage below.

How shall I begin to tell of the deeds wrought by these nefarious men! [the crusaders] Alas, the images, which ought to have been adored, were trodden under foot! Alas, the relics of the holy martyrs were thrown into unclean places! Then was seen what one shudders to hear, namely, the divine body and blood of Christ was spilled upon the ground or thrown about. They snatched the precious reliquaries, thrust into their bosoms the ornaments which these contained, and used the broken remnants for pans and drinking cups…
Nor can the violation of the Great Church [*Hagia Sophia*] be listened to with equanimity. For the sacred altar, formed of all kinds of precious materials and admired by the whole world, was broken into bits and distributed among the soldiers, as was all the other sacred wealth of so great and infinite splendor.

When the sacred vases and utensils of unsurpassable art and grace and rare material, and the fine silver, wrought with gold, which encircled the screen of the tribunal…and the door and many other ornaments, were to be [taken as spoils], mules and saddled horses were led to the very sanctuary of the temple. Some of these which were unable to keep their footing on the splendid and slippery pavement, were stabbed when they fell, so that the sacred pavement was polluted with blood and filth.

No one was without a share in the grief. In the alleys, in the streets, in the temples, complaints, weeping, lamentations, grief, the groaning of men, the shrieks of women, wounds, rape, captivity, the separation of those most closely united. Nobles wandered about ignominiously, those of venerable age in tears, the rich in poverty. Thus it was in the streets, on the corners, in the temple, in the dens, for no place remained unassailed or defended the suppliants. All places everywhere were filled full of all kinds of crime. Oh, immortal God, how great the afflictions of the men, how great the distress!

Nicetas Choniates, excerpt from *The Sack of Constantinople*, 1204

1. After reading the passage, what could a historian surmise about Constantinople in the 13th century?
   (A) The city was situated in a poorly protected location and was easily invaded.
   (B) The city was a rich and prosperous center of Christian faith.
   (C) The city was in decline having been sacked by the Mongols.
   (D) The city was the center of a thriving Muslim caliphate.

2. Why were the crusaders in the Byzantine Empire at this time?
   (A) They had arrived to aid the Byzantines fight against the increasing Mongol threat.
   (B) They had been sent by the pope to destroy Constantinople, the center of the Orthodox Church.
   (C) They were there to claim lands and trading rights for powerful merchants and church leaders.
   (D) They were on their way to the eastern shores of the Mediterranean to drive out the Muslims.

3. During the period 1200-1450, the fate of cities like Constantinople varied greatly, with periods of significant decline caused by not only invasions but also by which of the following?
    (A) unpreventable and misunderstood outbreaks of disease
    (B) the increase of agricultural productivity leading to demographic change
    (C) pollution of both air and waterways as production of manufacturing grew
    (D) population growth resulting in increasingly violent warfare

Questions 4-6 refer to the passage below.

Anyone from Genoa or from Venice, wishing … to make the journey to Cathay, should carry linens with him, and if he visits Organci [city in Central Asia] he will dispose of these well. In Organci he should purchase *sommi* (11 ounces) of silver, and with these he should proceed without making any further investment, unless it be some bales of the very finest stuffs which go in small bulk, and cost no more for carriage than coarser stuffs would do. Merchants who travel this road can ride on horseback or on asses or mounted in any way that they wish to be mounted.

Whatever silver the merchants may carry with them as far as Cathay the lord of Cathay will take from them and put into his treasury. And to merchants who thus bring silver they give that paper money of theirs in exchange. This is of yellow paper, stamped with the seal of the lord aforesaid….and with this money you can readily buy silk and all other merchandize that you have a desire to buy. And all the people of the country are bound to receive it. And yet you shall not pay a higher price for your goods because your money is of paper. And of the said paper money there are three kinds, one being worth more than another, according to the value which has been established for each by that lord.

And you may reckon that you can buy for one sommo of silver nineteen or twenty pounds of Cathay silk… You may reckon also that in Cathay you should get three or three and a half pieces of damasked silk for a sommo…

> Excerpt from a manuscript, *Pratica della Mercatura,* regarding the Eurasian trade, c. 1340

4. What could a historian learn from the excerpt concerning the economic situation in 14th century Eurasia?
 (A) There was little trade conducted between Venice and China at this time.
 (B) The Chinese valued the silver coinage of Europe.
 (C) The only luxury goods that were taken from China to Italy were silk textiles.
 (D) Goods went directly from China to Europe as there was no merchant activity in Central Asia.

5. What can be surmised about long distance trade in Eurasia by reading the excerpt?
 (A) Trade was sporadic and seasonal as it depended on climatic conditions.
 (B) It was too dangerous to carry luxury goods along the Silk Roads as bandits were common.
 (C) Trade between Europe and Asia was made possible by relatively peaceful conditions of the Silk Roads.
 (D) Most of the goods carried along the Silk Roads were of low value and so they were transported in bulk.

6. What was the impact of trans-regional trade in the period 1200 to 1450?
   (A) Existing trade routes flourished and promoted the growth of powerful new trading cities.
   (B) Spanish sponsorship of voyages across the Atlantic dramatically increased European interest in transoceanic trade.
   (C) There was a decrease in trade as epidemics caused the death of over half the population of Eurasia.
   (D) Trade by sea vastly outstripped overland trade because of new naval technology.

Questions 7-10 refer to the passages below.

Source 1

On the next day…the seamen began to make ready their boats, and to take out those captives [slaves], and carry them on shore. And these, placed all together in that field, were a marvelous sight; for amongst them were some white enough, fair to look upon, and well proportioned; others were less white like mulattoes; others again were as black as Ethiops, and so ugly, both in features and in body, as almost to appear (to those who saw them) the images of a lower hemisphere. But what heart could be so hard as not to be pierced with piteous feeling to see that company? For some kept their heads low and their faces bathed in tears, looking one upon another; others stood groaning very dolorously, looking up to the height of heaven, fixing their eyes upon it, crying out loudly, as if asking help of the Father of Nature; others struck their faces with the palms of their hands, throwing themselves at full length upon the ground; others made their lamentations in the manner of a dirge, after the custom of their country.

Gomes Eannes de Azurara, Portuguese chronicler, from *The Chronicle of the Discovery and Conquest of Guinea*, 1444

Source 2

Howbeit there is a most stately temple to be seen, the walls whereof are made of stone and lime; and a princely palace also built by a most excellent workman of Granada. Here are many shops of artificers, and merchants, and especially of such as weave linen and cotton cloth. And hither do the Barbary merchants bring cloth of Europe… The rich king of Timbuktu hath many plates and scepters of gold… He hath always three thousand horsemen, and a great number of footmen that shoot poisoned arrows, attending upon him….

Here are great store of doctors, judges, priests and other learned men, that are bountifully maintained at the kings cost and charges. And hither are brought diverse manuscripts or written books out of Barbary, which are sold for more money than any other merchandize.

Leo Africanus, diplomat and author, early 16th century

7. Which of the following best describes the chronicler's reaction to the slave trade that he witnessed in Source 1?
   (A) He was proud of the Portuguese power and regarded the slaves as a mere commodity.
   (B) He was shocked that the slaves appeared to not understand the Christian faith.
   (C) He was contemptuous of the slave traders whom he regarded as godless individuals.
   (D) He was moved by the wretched reaction of the slaves regardless of his belief in their inferiority.

8. Why did the Portuguese become heavily involved in the movement of African slaves during the 16th century?
   (A) Slaves were valuable as workers in the diamond mines of southern Africa.
   (B) Slaves were necessary for the growth of the plantation economy in the Americas.
   (C) The Portuguese needed deckhands to work on their caravels and carracks as they extended their power.
   (D) Slaves were increasingly popular as domestic servants in the homes of rich European elite.

9. What does the second passage reveal about Timbuktu in the 16th century?
   (A) It was a place of pilgrimage in the Saharan region.
   (B) It was a lawless city that was prone to violence.
   (C) It was the center of cultural diffusion.
   (D) It was a Muslim enclave where other religions were discouraged.

10. How had Timbuktu developed into the city that Leo Africanus describes?
    (A) It was a center of Portuguese activity and had developed as a slaving center.
    (B) It was situated on an important trans-Saharan trade route.
    (C) It was situated on the west coast of Africa and developed rapidly because of its safe harbor.
    (D) It was the only city in this part of west Africa untouched by the Black Death.

Questions 11-13 refer to the image below.

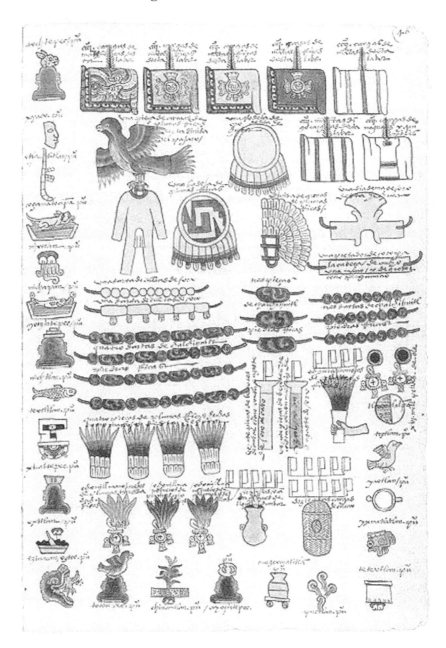

The image above is an illustration from the Codex Mendoza, *an Aztec account of the tribute towns were required to pay to the Aztec Empire, c. 1542.*

11. A historian would most likely use this image to illustrate which of the following?
    (A) The importance of exotic plumage in the military power structure
    (B) The lack of domesticable animals in Central America that enabled the Spanish to achieve easy victory
    (C) The low rate of literacy in the Central America, and the consequent need for pictorial records
    (D) The methods used by the Aztec to generate revenue for territorial expansion

12. The image can best be used as evidence for which of the following world historical trends that took place during the period 1200 to 1750?
   (A) The diffusion of American cultural traditions into Europe
   (B) The use of art to glorify rulers
   (C) The use of intimidation to ensure territorial control
   (D) States' use of military power to foster nationalism

13. Which of the following statements best explains the historical process evident in the imperial system created by the Mexica (Aztecs)?
   (A) The Aztec Empire was like the Abbasid Caliphate in Eurasia as it was centered around the growth of education and scholarly investigation.
   (B) The Aztec Empire was like the Mayan city-states in that it relied on previously existing trade networks that connected much of Mesoamerica.
   (C) The Aztec Empire was the foundation for the concept of a Gran Colombia that was championed by Simón Bolivar in the early 19th century.
   (D) The Aztec Empire was larger in size that the Roman Empire due to the superior organization of the Aztec warriors.

Questions 14-16 refer to the image below.

The image above depicts a painting of Japanese Samurai warriors in battle, 16th century.

14. What could a historian learn about Medieval Japan from studying the image?
    (A) Japan was a highly centralized state with a powerful imperial army
    (B) The Japanese were fierce warriors with advanced military technology.
    (C) The Japanese were able to defend themselves from their powerful neighbor China.
    (D) Japanese society was highly stratified and rigid in the 16th century.

15. Which of the following comparisons best describes the relationship between the knights of feudal Europe and the samurai warriors of feudal Japan?
    (A) European knights were more effective as they had suits of armor made of metal Whereas those of the samurai were made of leather.
    (B) European knights and samurai warriors were both soldiers who pledged their loyalty to their lord at a time of decentralized government.
    (C) European knights took directives from religious leaders like the pope, whereas the samurai had no religious affiliation.
    (D) Both European knights and samurai warriors had a code of behavior that mandated they commit suicide if they violated the code in any way.

16. Which of the following best describes the Japanese economy during the feudal period?
    (A) Japan was an agricultural society based on the production of rice.
    (B) Chinampas were created to increase the amount of arable land.
    (C) The Japanese economy was centered around long-distance trade.
    (D) A high level of industrialization in Japan put them at the forefront of car manufacturing.

Questions 17-19 refer to the images below.

Source 1

The image above depicts the Süleymaniye Mosque, constructed in Istanbul during the reign of Süleyman, c.1550.

Source 2

The image above depicts the Red Fort, constructed in Delhi during the reign of Shah Jahan, c. 1639.

17. Which of the following statements is correct when describing the two images above?
    (A) They were both created to celebrate military victories.
    (B) They both portray blended Islamic elements and elements of the local culture.
    (C) They were built as religious symbols of the power of the Mughal and Ottoman empires.
    (D) They were both built by coerced labor that was used to intimidate the subject people.

18. Why did rulers like Süleyman and Shah Jahan construct monumental architecture in the period 1450 to 1750?
    (A) They were trying to legitimize their rule in large diverse empires.
    (C) They were trying to accommodate the different ethnic and religious groups of their subjects by adopting a progressive style of architecture.
    (D) They were attempting to create a common belief system in order to unite their subjects.
    (E) They were aiming to ensure a high level of employment and thus avoid rebellions.

19. Which of the following is most comparable to the actions of Süleyman and Shah Jahan?
    (A) The Nazi party organized an attack on the Reichstag building in Berlin in 1933 to gain support.
    (B) Guy Fawkes and a group of Catholics attempted to blow up the Parliament in London in 1605.
    (C) Louis XIV expanded his father's hunting lodge to build the Palace of Versailles in the 17th and 18th centuries.
    (D) The Japanese built an artificial island in Nagasaki bay to enable trade with Portuguese and Dutch merchants in 1634.

Questions 20-23 refer to the passage below.

Apart from the other tax burdens which the Christians had to bear under [Ottoman] Turkish rule, from time to time their handsomest offspring were seized from them. Separating the children from their parents, the Turks would instruct them in the martial arts. These children, abducted by force, never returned to their parents. Alienated from the Christian religion, little by little they forgot faith, parents, brothers and sisters, and all their blood relatives, so that when they later encountered their parents they no longer even recognized them.

I can find no right words to picture the pain and sorrow, the weeping and wailing of these parents when their children are torn from their bosoms and out of their grasp by those fiends. To parents who had just barely begun to instruct their children in Christian teaching, the hardest thought was that the evildoers would soon succeed in seducing them away from the religion of their forebears and in turning them into dreadful enemies of the Christian religion and Christian people.

  Bartholomew Georgiewitz, Hungarian who spent 13 years as a Turkish slave, 16th century

20. According to the author, what was the long-term result of the abduction of young children by the Ottoman Turks?
    (A) As they grew older, the children learned to practice both Christianity and Islam.
    (B) Very few of the children survived the brutal seizure by the Ottomans.
    (C) The children were able to profit from their new situation and often became important members of the Ottoman Empire.
    (D) The children adopted Islamic culture and remained distant from their Christian roots.

21. Which of the following best explains why the Ottomans used children from the Christian regions in their army and bureaucracy?
    (A) Christian children were raised by their parents to be more compliant than those of Muslim families.
    (B) Christian children were better educated than those of the nomadic Ottoman culture.
    (C) The children grew up with a strong devotion to the Ottoman rulers as they owed no other allegiance.
    (D) The bubonic plague had decimated the Ottoman population and there were insufficient young people.

22. Which of the following describes how a different empire in this period was able to recruit bureaucrats?
    (A) Queen Isabella of Spain's recruitment of Jewish scribes to work in the *cortes*
    (B) the Chinese reliance on the Confucian civil service exam to recruit a bureaucratic elite
    (C) The Mughal incorporation of Buddhist scribes as bureaucrats in local government offices
    (D) The French governments employment of Huguenot administrators in regional *parlements*

23. The Janissaries were ultimately a factor in the decline of the Ottoman empire because…
    (A) they eventually returned to their original Christian beliefs and revolted.
    (B) of the many defeats they suffered in battle during the final years of the empire.
    (C) their leaders became corrupt and sought political power for themselves.
    (D) many of the soldiers refused to use the new rifle bullets that were coated with pig and cow fat.

Questions 24-26 refer to the passage below.

Very dear and well beloved: Considering how advantageous it would be to this realm to reestablish its foreign and domestic commerce ... we have resolved to establish a council particularly devoted to commerce, to be held every fortnight in our presence, in which all the interests of merchants and the means conducive to the revival of commerce shall be considered and determined upon, as well as all that which concerns manufactures.

We also inform you that we are setting apart, in the expenses of our state, a million livres* each year for the encouragement of manufactures and the increase of navigation, to say nothing of the considerable sums which we cause to be raised to supply the companies of the East and West Indies…

*a livre was the value of one pound of silver

A letter from Louis XIV to the People of Marseilles, 1664

24. According to the passage, what change did Louis XIV attempt to make to the French economy in the late 17th century?
    (A) He increased tariffs on foreign goods in order to increase the state's wealth through taxation.
    (B) He adopted an isolationist policy that protected France from competition by foreign merchants.
    (C) He advocated a rapid industrialization process in order to catch up with British developments.
    (D) He encouraged the development of profitable local and foreign trading.

25. Louis' economic policies resulted in which of the following?
    (A) the creation of an industrialized state that dominated Europe
    (B) the expansion of French colonial holdings in Asia and the Americas
    (C) the persecution of the protestant Huguenots and Jews of France
    (D) a series of conflicts with the English which culminated in a hundred years of warfare

26. Which of the following was most important long-term effect of Western European economic policy in the 17th and 18th century?
    (A) There was increased tension among European powers which resulted in a series of military disputes world-wide.
    (B) Trading agreements were made between France and Spain in order to isolate the British.
    (C) The average income of merchants rose dramatically, and patronage of the arts increased in most parts of Europe.
    (D) An increase in interregional and global trade networks facilitated the spread of religion and other elements of culture.

Questions 27-29 refer to the passage below.

"A great peace is at hand. The shogun rules firmly and with justice at Edo. No more shall we have to live by the sword. I have seen that great profit can be made honorably. I shall brew sake and soy sauce and we shall prosper."

                                                                     Mitsui Takatoshi, merchant, 1670

27. Based on the text, which social stratum was the impetus [reason] for Japan's commercial expansion?
    (A) the power of the daimyo in the provinces
    (B) the commercialization of the Japanese economy by the emperor
    (C) the enterprise of the merchant class in a peaceful political era
    (D) the ingenuity of large business conglomerates known as *zaibatsu*

28. Why did Tokugawa Japan have limited trade with European nations?
    (A) European merchants were unwilling to travel to Japan's isolated location.
    (B) Japan did not have resources that were desired by Europeans.
    (C) Japan felt threatened by the growing influence of Europe in the Pacific region.
    (D) The Europeans had nothing of interest for the Japanese.

29. The Tokugawa restricted trade and only had regular commercial contact with…
    (A) Britain Belgium, and France.
    (B) China, Korea, and The Netherlands.
    (C) The United States.
    (D) Russia and Vietnam.

Questions 30-32 refer to the passages below.

Source 1

Mothers, daughters, sisters, female representatives of the nation ask to be constituted as a national assembly.

Considering that ignorance, neglect, or contempt for the rights of woman are the sole causes of public misfortunes and governmental corruption, they have resolved to set forth in a solemn declaration the natural, inalienable, and sacred rights of woman: so that by being constantly present to all the members of the social body this declaration may always remind them of their rights and duties…

> Olympe de Gouges, *The Declaration of the Rights of Woman*, 1791

Source 2

My own sex, I hope, will excuse me, if I treat them like rational creatures, instead of flattering their fascinating graces, and viewing them as if they were in a state of perpetual childhood, unable to stand alone.

> Mary Wollstonecraft, *A Vindication of the Rights of Woman*, 1792

30. What was the historical situation that led Olympe de Gouges make her declaration?
    (A) The patriarchal nature of French society had resulted in the prosecution of numerous women accused of witchcraft.
    (B) The Third Estate in France had created a new political institution which had created a decree which defined individual and collective rights.
    (C) Louis XVI had passed a law that placed new restrictions on women's rights to own property.
    (D) Jean-Paul Marat had written a series of editorials in his periodical *L'Ami du Peuple* criticizing the desire of French women to be considered equal to men.

31. Wollstonecraft's late 18th century message to women shows which point of view?
    (A) She thought women were to be treated as ornaments to society.
    (B) She did not believe women should have an education as it would be wasted on them.
    (C) She maintained that women should only receive a domestic education.
    (D) She felt that there was a sexual standard that encouraged women to indulge in excessive emotion.

32. Which of the following statements concerning Mary Wollstonecraft and Olympe de Gouges is correct?
    (A) They were revolutionaries who advocated democracy and the overthrow of monarchy.
    (B) They, like Pan Chao in Han China, said that women belonged in the home.
    (C) They believed that philosophic salons created a conduit for the exchange of information between women.
    (D) They were early advocates of giving women the same chances as men.

Questions 33 - 35 refer to the image below.

The image above depicts a painting by François-René Moreau, titled Announcement of Independence, *painted in 1844.*

33. What does the artist hope to achieve through this rendering of the day Pedro I declared the independence of Brazil in 1822?
    (A) He desires to show the respect that the people of Brazil have for King Pedro I.
    (B) He wants to portray how the people of Brazil have broken away from any European style culture.
    (C) He wishes to illustrate how united the people of Brazil are in their desire for independence from Portugal.
    (D) He tries to prove that the army of Brazil backed the idea of independence wholeheartedly.

34. Which of the following statements describes the **major** difference between the way Brazil achieved independence and the way other states of Latin South America became independent?
    (A) Brazil did not end its colonial status until late in the 19th century, whereas the Spanish states had all achieved independence by the mid-century.
    (B) Creoles incited and led slave rebellions in Brazil, but *mestizos* were the driving force in the Spanish colonies of Latin America.
    (C) Brazilian independence was achieved with less violence and Brazil became a monarchy, whereas the Spanish states converted into republics.
    (D) Slaves led uprisings in Brazil and in Haiti but not in the Spanish empire's holdings.

35. Why was the abolition of slavery achieved so much later in Brazil than in other parts of the Americas?
    (A) The small size of the Brazilian population made slavery an economic necessity.
    (B) Brazil was economically independent from the rest of the world and therefore was unaffected by abolitionist sentiments.
    (C) The Brazilian government refused to cooperate with more progressive American and European governments.
    (D) There were more slaves in Brazil than anywhere else in the Americas as sugar exports were the mainstay of the economy.

Questions 36-38 refer to the passage below.

One day toward the end of January last, a workman employed in the magazine at Barrackpore, an important station about seventeen miles from Calcutta, stopped to ask a Sepoy for some water from his drinking-vessel. Being refused, because he was of low caste, and his touch would defile the vessel, he said, with a sneer, "What caste are you of, who bite pig's grease and cow's fat on your cartridges?" Practice with the new Enfield rifle had just been introduced, and the cartridges were greased for use in order not to foul the gun. The rumor spread among the Sepoys that there was a trick played upon them, – that this was but a device to pollute them and destroy their caste, and the first step toward a general and forcible conversion of the soldiers to Christianity.

Charles Creighton Hazewell, "The Indian Revolt," *The Atlantic Monthly*, 1857

36. What could a historian studying the passage conclude about the socio-cultural characteristics of India in the 19th century?
    (A) There was an ongoing attempt by the government powers to create equality in Indian society.
    (B) There was a deep tension between Hindus and Muslims in India based on religious differences.
    (C) The Indian people felt threatened by the power of the British in South Asia.
    (D) Dietary restrictions led to distrust between the religious groups in India.

37. What was the outcome of the Indian Revolt that the author described in the magazine?
    (A) The Indian people were able to force the British government to start negotiations for the independence of India.
    (B) The British withdrew most of their troops from Indian soil and gave the Indians more autonomy.
    (C) The British government imposed direct rule on India, replacing the British East India Company.
    (D) The British East India company stopped using local sepoy soldiers in their armies and instead recruited British mercenary soldiers.

38. What was the main reason that the British colonized South Asia in the 18th and 19th centuries?
    (A) The British wanted to build factories in India to take advantage of its cheap labor.
    (B) The British sought raw materials and new markets for the increasing amount and array of goods produced in their factories.
    (C) The British needed Indian rice to increase food supplies for the growing population in urban centers.
    (D) The British planned to integrate India into the global economy as an industrial and economic hub.

Questions 39-40 refer to the image below.

EMIGRATION TO SOUTH AUSTRALIA

Her Majesty's Colonization Commissioners having determined to dispatch in the course of a few weeks a large number of Emigrants, all eligible persons may obtain, by making an IMMEDIATE application, a

FREE PASSAGE!

The classes of persons now in requisition are
Agricultural Laborers,
SHEPHERDS, CARPENTERS
BLACKSMITHS
AND
STONE MASONS
And all Persons connected with Building.
Application to be made to
Mr. L. LATIMER,
Rosewin-row, TRURO.

The image above depicts a poster printed in England, 1870.

39. What was the main reason the British government was encouraging the emigration from Britain to Australia in the late 19th century?
    (A) The government feared uprisings among the working people of large urban areas threatened by the growing popularity of Communism.
    (B) The government was looking for solutions to the income gap between the wealthy investors and the urban workers.
    (C) The government was attempting to ease unemployment and improve its finances by creating flourishing economies in its overseas territories.
    (D) The government was reacting to a pandemic of influenza that had struck southern Britain.

40. Australia was considered a settler colony. What was the most important difference between settler colonies and other transregional colonies?
    (A) In settler colonies land ownership was paramount, whereas natural and human resources were the main motivation behind other forms of colonialism.
    (B) Settler colonies had larger populations than other colonies.
    (C) Settler colonies were more important than other colonies in providing important raw materials needed in industrialized mother nations.
    (D) Settler colonies were created in regions that were barren and unpopulated, whereas other forms of colonialism developed in densely populated regions with fertile land.

Questions 41-43 refer to the passages below.

Source 1

Whites have clearly come out on top in the struggle for existence and achieved the highest standard of human existence. Therefore, I shall devote the rest of my life to God's purpose and help him make the world English.

Cecil Rhodes, "Confession of Faith" in 1876

Source 2

Can we hammer civilization into savage minds by sheer force? Have we any proof that such policy has been largely successful? Will the conquest of Zululand which is almost certain to be achieved be followed by results of which modern civilization can boast? Are we to fight our way through Africa or shall we win it?

Excerpt from an editorial in the *Illustrated London News* during the Zulu Rebellion, 1879

41. What justification did Cecil Rhodes use to validate the expansion of existing overseas empires and the establishment of new colonies?
    (A) He felt that Social Darwinism had resulted in the superiority of some civilizations over others.
    (B) He believed that it was necessary to spread Christianity to the pagan people of the world.
    (C) He understood that the Industrial Revolution created the need for new territories to provide raw materials for European factories.
    (D) He believed that it was necessary to ensure that the British Empire was more powerful than that of the French.

42. What is the political/philosophical basis of the argument expounded in the editorial?
    (A) the belief that all men are created equal and should share equal rights
    (B) the doubt that religion could be used to explain human action as cruelty is ever present
    (C) the socialist belief that promoted a controlled economy run for the benefit of all
    (D) the principle that violent control of one cultural group over another was not justified

43. The revolt of the Zulu Kingdom was an example of anti-imperial resistance. Which of the following is another example of anti-imperial resistance?
    (A) the American overthrow of the Hawaiian monarchy in 1893
    (B) the Fashoda Incident in 1898
    (C) the Chinese Boxer Rebellion in 1899
    (D) the Moroccan Crisis in 1905

Questions 44-46 refer to the passage below.

The Brazilian Nation, which has never engaged in a war of conquest, but has consistently advocated arbitration as the solution for external conflicts...

Brazil, therefore, recognizes that ...the restoration of France and Italy should be granted, and the Balkan problem and the restitution of liberty to Poland be considered.

Through the sufferings and the disillusions to which the war has given rise a new and better world will be born, as it were, of liberty, and in this way a lasting peace may be established without political or economic restrictions, and all countries be allowed a place in the sun with equal rights and an interchange of ideas and values in merchandise on an ample basis of justice and equity.

> Dr. Nilo Pecanha, Brazil's Foreign Minister, from a letter to the Brazilian Ambassador to Pope Benedict, October 1917

44. According to the excerpt, which of the following is supported by the Brazilians?
    (A) The Catholic Church has the moral obligation to impose order in Europe.
    (B) The ideas of the Enlightenment should be encouraged to spread.
    (C) The sovereignty of national borders should be respected by all nations.
    (D) Germany should be punished at the peace conference following the war.

45. The Brazilian government's attitude is most aligned with what other post World War I position?
    (A) the League of Nations' order to dismantle the Mandate system
    (B) Lenin's communist proposal of "Peace, Land, and Bread"
    (C) the Treaty of Versailles' War Guilt Clause blaming Germany for World War I
    (D) U.S. President Wilson's idea of self-determination presented in the Fourteen Points

46. The international attempt to solve multi-national problems in 1917 is most like...
    (A) the Treaty of Paris granting independence to the United States after the Revolutionary War.
    (B) the Seneca Falls Conventions seeking international recognition of women's rights.
    (C) the creation of the Triple Entente and the Triple Alliance prior to World War I.
    (D) the Congress of Vienna's attempt to restore order after the Napoleonic Wars.

Questions 47-49 refer to the passages below.

Source 1

Auschwitz is actually a reception center for political prisoners, for those 'in protective custody.' In April 1942, at the time of my assignment there, there were about 15,000 prisoners, mostly Poles, German nationals, and Russian civilians. ...All prisoners come first to Auschwitz, where they are provided with appropriate numbers; they are either kept there or are sent to Birkenau; only a few go to Harmansee. Prisoners are allotted numbers in the order of their admittance. Numbers are used only once, so that the last number shows the total number of prisoners admitted up to that date. At the time of our escape from Birkenau, at the beginning of April 1944, this [highest] number was about 180,000. Numbers were at first tattooed on the left breast, but later, as these numbers became illegible, on the left arm above the wrist.

Alfred Wetzler and Rudolf Vrba, two escapees from Auschwitz, 1944

Source 2

Also from 1975, money was abolished and big houses were either demolished, and the materials used for smaller ones, or used for administration or to house troops. The banana trees in the fields were all uprooted on the orders of the Khmer Rouge and rice planted in their place. Production was high, although some land was left fallow and rations usually just consisted of rice porridge with very little meat. After the harvest each year, trucks would come at night to take away the village's rice stores to an unknown destination. In 1975, the Khmer Rouge also began executing rich people, although they spared the elderly owner of 800 hectares. They also executed college students and former government officials, soldiers and police. I saw the bodies of many such people not far from the village.

Thoun Cheng, a Cambodian refugee who fled the Pol Pot regime in 1977

47. What direct evidence of inhumane treatment is portrayed in the first document?
    (A) Overcrowded and unsanitary conditions were the norm in Polish camps.
    (B) Guards separated Poles from Germans and Russians in order to prevent collaboration.
    (C) The authorities dehumanized prisoners by treating them as if they were commodities.
    (D) The security at the Polish camps was so efficient that escape was rare.

48. Which example is most similar to the agricultural policy of the Khmer Rouge?
    (A) the "Battle for Grain" undertaken by the Fascists in Italy during the 1920s
    (B) the Collectivization program carried out in Soviet Russia under Stalin
    (C) the Corn Laws enacted by the British government in the early 19th century
    (D) the Enclosure movement that drove peasants off the land in the 16th century

49. What was the underlying reason that actions like those in the two excerpts increased in the 20th century?
    (A) There was more competition for habitable land as the world population doubled between 1900 and 2000.
    (B) The migration of former colonial subjects to imperial metropoles led to anger against immigrants.
    (C) Following World War I and the onset of the Great Depression, governments began to take a more active role in citizens' lives.
    (D) Political changes led to the rise of extremist groups in power who targeted specific populations.

Questions 50-53 refer to the chart below.

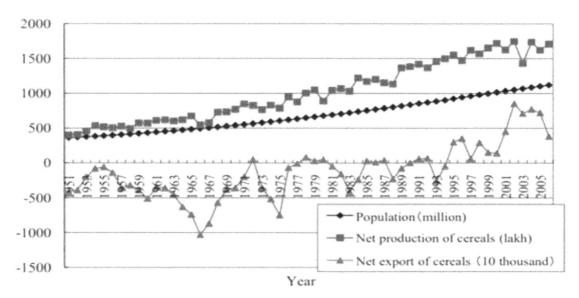

Population and Cereal Production & Trade in India

50. Which of the following best explains the overall demographic trend shown in the chart?
    (A) There was very little change in the total population of India between 1950 and 2000.
    (B) The export of cereals from India reflects a similar pattern in the export of cereals from the United States in the same period.
    (C) As the population of India grew there was an equivalent growth in the production of cereals.
    (D) The monsoon winds that bring rain to the Indian subcontinent allow agriculture to flourish.

51. Which of the following best describes the Indian government's response to the demographic trend shown on the chart?
    (A) They passed a one-child law that was aimed at reducing the population growth rate.
    (B) They took no legislative action as one of the basic tenets of Indian philosophy is living in harmony with nature.
    (C) In marginalized communities, they encouraged abortion as the prime method to reduce the birth rate.
    (D) They encouraged rapid advances in science and technology to make advances in agriculture.

52. How did the earlier actions of the Chinese Communist Party in the Great Leap Forward differ from those of the Indian government in the Green Revolution of the 1960s and 1970s?
    (A) The Chinese were more successful in increasing crop yields than the Indians.
    (B) The Great Leap Forward was designed to lead to rapid industrialization whereas the Indian government focused on agriculture.
    (C) The Great Leap Forward was planned to reduce the Chinese population whereas the Green Revolution encouraged larger families.
    (D) The Great Leap Forward was more scientifically based than the Green Revolution.

53. What was the aim of the Green Revolution in the mid-20th century?
    (A) to reduce population growth in the developing world as birth control efforts proved ineffective
    (B) to increase agricultural production in the developing world to sustain growing populations
    (C) to diminish social inequalities in the developing world in order to avoid civil rebellions and ensure international peace
    (D) to combat soil pollution in the developing world by moderating the use of chemical fertilizers

Questions 54 - 55 refer to the charts below.

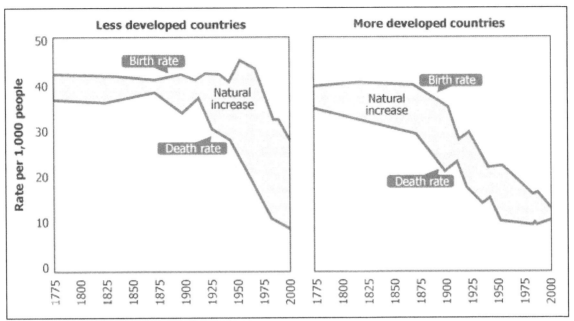

Human Population: Future Growth," Population Reference Bureau, 2015.

54. Which of the following is a major cause of the changes indicated in the charts?
    (A) Modern warfare was responsible for overall population loss.
    (B) Women entering the workforce had less time to care for the family.
    (C) Poor living conditions in crowded tenements in urban areas led to decreases in population.
    (D) Scientific advancement like birth control and penicillin lowered both death and birth rates.

55. One result of the population trends depicted in the charts is…
    (A) increased strain on natural resources in less developed countries.
    (B) populations in more developed countries whose average age is younger than in previous years.
    (C) labor migration from former colonizing countries to former colonies.
    (D) increased access to education in less developed countries.

SHORT-ANSWER QUESTIONS

SAQ Directions:

There are four short-answer questions (SAQs) on the exam. Together, they account for 20% of your total exam score. This section contains four sets of four SAQs—one set for each time period covered in AP World History: Modern. The ideal way to use this section is to practice SAQs throughout the year, as you progress through each period of history in class.

In order to prepare for the exam, it is best to replicate exam conditions whenever you practice. For writing SAQs, set a timer for 40 minutes and then proceed to answer Question 1, Question 2, and **either** Question 3 **or** Question 4 in a chosen set. Make sure to limit the length of your responses so that all three parts of the question (a, b, and c) are answered on a single side of lined paper. Write in pen (no whiteout!).

When you are finished, check your answers using the key in the back, which features annotated samples of acceptable responses.

COMMON MISTAKES (doing any of these will disqualify your response)	WHAT TO DO INSTEAD
not demonstrating the tested skill	-If the prompt refers to the stimulus, you are being tested on your primary/secondary source analysis skills. Make sure to refer to the relevant part of the stimulus in your response. -If the prompt asks about a similarity or difference, you are being tested on your comparison skills. Make sure to explain BOTH topics in your response in a way that displays what they have in common or how they differ. -If the prompt asks about a continuity or a change, you are being tested on your CCOT skills. For a continuity, use wording that demonstrates the passing of time (*throughout*, *during*, etc.). For a change, make sure to use words that indicate change (*before*, *after*, etc.).
using vague statements or universal truisms	You must show that you know about a specific time in history. Use the wording from the prompt to narrow down the focus of your response, then be as specific as possible in your explanation. If your response could also be true for any other time or place in history, it won't earn credit!
responding in incomplete sentences	Write in complete sentences. Do not use bullet points.

Set 1: 1200 to 1450 Secondary Source

Use the passage below to answer all parts of the question that follows.

> "Many people think that because [the Mongols] were nomads they must have been barbarians. But this is a mistaken idea. They did not know, of course, many of the city arts, but they had developed a way of life of their own and had an intricate organization....
>
> If they won great victories on the field of battle, it was not because of their numbers, but because of their discipline and organization. And above all it was due to the brilliant captain-ship of Chinggis....Western Europe saved itself from the Mongols not by any valour of its own, but by the indifference and the preoccupations of the Mongols....
>
> In the course of our wanderings through past ages we have seen many invasions of Europe by Asia. There were some invasions of Asia by Europe, but they were of little moment. Alexander went across Asia to India without any great result. The Romans never went beyond Mesopotamia. Europe, on the other hand, was repeatedly overrun by Asiatic tribes from the earliest times. It is well to remember this, as some people, ignorant of history, imagine that Europe has always bossed it over Asia...."
>
> -Jawaharlal Nehru, activist for Indian independence from Great Britain, from letters written to his daughter from jail between 1930-1933, later published as *Glimpses of World History* in 1942

1. a) Provide ONE piece of historical evidence that supports Nehru's argument in the <u>second paragraph</u>.

   b) Explain ONE historical example of an Asiatic group, other than the Mongols, that invaded Europe.

   c) Explain ONE factor that likely shaped Nehru's view of the Mongols.

Set 1: 1200 to 1450 Primary Source

Use the passage below to answer all parts of the question that follows.

"Their women are of surpassing beauty, and are shown more respect than the men. The state of affairs amongst these people is indeed extraordinary. Their men show no signs of jealousy whatever; no one claims descent from his father, but on the contrary from his mother's brother. A person's heirs are his sister's sons, not his own sons. This is a thing which I have seen nowhere in the world except among the Indians of Malabar. But those are heathens; these people are Muslims, punctilious in observing the hours of prayer, studying books of law, and memorizing the Koran. Yet their women show no bashfulness before men and do not veil themselves, though they are assiduous in attending the prayers. Any man who wishes to marry one of them may do so, but they do not travel with their husbands, and even if one desired to do so her family would not allow her to go.

The women there have "friends" and "companions" amongst the men outside their own families, and the men in the same way have "companions" amongst the women of other families. A man may go into his house and find his wife entertaining her "companion" but he takes no objection to it. One day at Walata I went into the qadi's [Islamic judge] house, after asking his permission to enter, and found with him a young woman of remarkable beauty. When I saw her I was shocked and turned to go out, but she laughed at me, instead of being overcome by shame, and the qadi said to me "Why are you going out? She is my companion." I was amazed at their conduct, for he was a theologian and a pilgrim [to Mecca] to boot. I was told that he had asked the sultan's permission to make the pilgrimage that year with his "companion"—whether this one or not I cannot say—but the sultan would not grant it."

-Description of the people of Walata (city in West Africa) written by Ibn Battuta, Muslim qadi and traveler, c. 1360

2. a) Explain ONE <u>social</u> continuity in West Africa in the period circa 1200-1450.

   b) Explain ONE <u>cultural</u> change in West Africa in the period circa 1200-1450.

   c) Explain ONE <u>economic</u> change in West Africa in the period circa 1200-1450.

Set 1: 1200 to 1450 No Stimulus

Directions: Answer **either** Question 3 **or** Question 4.
Answer all parts of the question that follows.

3. a) Explain ONE similarity between military technology in the Americas and in East Asia during 1200-1450.

   b) Explain ONE difference between military technology in the Americas and in East Asia during 1200-1450.

   c) Explain ONE reason for the difference between military technology in the Americas and in East Asia during 1200-1450.

Answer all parts of the question that follows.

4. a) Explain ONE similarity between the Silk Road and Indian Ocean trade routes.

   b) Explain ANOTHER similarity between the Silk Road and Indian Ocean trade routes.

   c) Explain ONE difference between the Silk Road and Indian Ocean trade routes.

Set 2: 1450 to 1750 Secondary Source

Use the passage below to answer all parts of the question that follows.

"The linkages that did exist [in the fifteenth century], especially in the Indian Ocean, were for the most part mutually agreeable and peaceful. No one part of the world attempted to seize or impose control over the whole system, even though the expansion of Islam in the seventh and eighth centuries did result in the conversion of huge numbers of people to that religion. The fifteenth-century voyages of Admiral Zheng He briefly extended Chinese influence over much of the Indian Ocean. The world was polycentric, with three major regions centered around China, India, and the Islamic world, and others connected to one or more of those powerhouses."

-Robert B. Marks, *The Origins of the Modern World: A Global and Environmental Narrative*, 2007

1. a) Explain ONE way the global economy described in the passage above changed during the time period 1450-1750.

   b) Explain ANOTHER way the global economy in the passage above changed during the time period 1450-1750.

   c) Explain ONE <u>reaction</u> in East Asia to changes in the global economy during the time period 1450-1750.

Set 2: 1450 to 1750 Primary Source

Use the images below to answer all parts of the question that follows.

Image 1

Ruins of the emperor's palace, *Panch Mahal*, in Fatehpur Sikri. Fatehpur Sikri was constructed under Emperor Ahkbar the Great and served as the Mughal capital city from 1571-1585.

Image 2

Peterhof Palace in St. Petersburg. St. Petersburg was constructed by Russian Tsar Peter the Great and served as Russia's capital city from 1713 until the 20th century.

2. a) Explain ONE similarity in how Peter the Great and Akbar the Great legitimized their rule, as reflected in the images above.

b) Explain ANOTHER similarity in how Peter the Great and Akbar the Great legitimized their rule.

c) Explain ONE difference in how Peter the Great and Akbar the Great maintained political power.

Set 2: 1450 to 1750 No Stimulus

Directions: Answer **either** Question 3 **or** Question 4.
Answer all parts of the question that follows.

3. a) Explain ONE economic change in the Americas in the period 1450-1750.

   b) Explain ONE cultural change in the Americas in the period 1450-1750.

   c) Explain ONE political change in the Americas in the period 1450-1750.

Answer all parts of the question that follows.

4. a) Explain ONE economic change in Europe in the period 1450-1750.

   b) Explain ONE cultural change in Europe in the period 1450-1750.

   c) Explain ONE political change in Europe in the period 1450-1750.

Set 3: 1750 to 1900 Secondary Source

Use the passage below to answer all parts of the question that follows.

> "We Americans like to think of our revolution as not being radical; indeed, most of the time we consider it downright conservative. It certainly does not appear to resemble the revolutions of other nations in which people were killed, property was destroyed, and everything was turned upside down. The American revolutionary leaders do not fit our conventional image of revolutionaries—angry, passionate, reckless, maybe even bloodthirsty for the sake of a cause....
>
> If we measure the radicalism of revolutions by the degree of social misery or economic deprivation suffered, or by the number of people killed or manor houses burned, then this conventional emphasis on the conservatism of the American Revolution becomes true enough. But if we measure the radicalism by the amount of social change that actually took place—by the transformations in the relationships that bound people to each other—then the American Revolution [of the Thirteen British Colonies] was not conservative at all; on the contrary: it was as radical and no less social for being different. In fact, it was one of the greatest revolutions the world has known, a momentous upheaval that not only fundamentally altered the character of American society but decisively affected the course of subsequent history."
>
> -Gordon S. Wood, historian, *The Radicalism of the American Revolution*, 1993

1. a) Provide ONE piece of historical evidence that would support Wood's argument in the <u>second paragraph</u>.

   b) Provide ONE piece of historical evidence that would challenge Wood's argument in the <u>second paragraph</u>.

   c) Provide ONE revolution that Wood is most likely referring to when depicting "revolutions in other nations" in the <u>first paragraph</u>.

Set 3: 1750 to 1900 Primary Source

Use the passage below to answer all parts of the question that follows.

"The most approved Judges of the Commercial Interests of these Kingdoms have been of the opinion that our West-Indian and African Trades are the most nationally beneficial of any we carry on…That Traffic alone affords our Planters a constant supply of [Black] Servants for the Culture of their Lands in the produce of Sugars, Tobacco, Rice, Rum, Cotton, Pimento and all our other Plantation Produce: so that the extensive Employment of our other Shipping in, to and from America, the great Brood of Seamen consequent thereupon, and the daily bread of the most considerable of our British Manufactures, are owing primarily to the Labour of [Black Slaves]."

-pamphlet published in London, 1749

2. a) Explain ONE way the passage above reflects an economic continuity since 1550.

   b) Explain ONE reason why the labor system mentioned in the passage above was abolished by Britain in the 19th century.

   c) Explain ANOTHER economic change in Britain during the period 1750-1900.

Set 3: 1750 to 1900 No Stimulus

Directions: Answer **either** Question 3 **or** Question 4.
Answer all parts of the question that follows.

3. a) Describe ONE similarity between European imperialism in Australia and European imperialism in Central Africa.

   b) Describe ONE difference between European imperialism in Australia and European imperialism in Central Africa.

   c) Explain ONE reason for the difference between European imperialism in Australia and European imperialism in Central Africa.

Answer all parts of the question that follows.

4. a) Describe ONE similarity between industrialization in Russia and industrialization in Japan during the period 1750-1900.

   b) Describe ONE difference between industrialization in Russia and industrialization in Japan during the period 1750-1900.

   c) Explain ONE reason for the difference between industrialization in Russia and industrialization in Japan during the period 1750-1900.

Set 4: 1900 to 2001 Secondary Source

Use the passage below to answer all parts of the question that follows.

"The term *Coca-Colonization* was first used by communist sympathizers in France, who mounted a vigorous campaign against the establishment of new bottling plants in their country. It would, they suggested, harm the domestic wine and mineral-water industries; they even tried to have Coca-Cola outlawed on the grounds that it was poisonous. This caused an outcry in America...The French papers responded in kind: *Le Monde* warned that "the moral landscape of France is at stake."... Ultimately, the French campaign against Coca-Cola made little difference. Indeed, it generated huge amounts of free publicity and gave the drink an exotic, illicit cachet....

The big new [market] is China. But that is just one of the more than two hundred territories where the Coca-Cola Company operates—more than the United Nations has members. Its drink is now the world's most widely known product, and "Coca-Cola" is said to be the second most commonly understood phrase in the world, after "OK." No other company can match it for global reach, visibility, or recognition. Coca-Cola consistently tops the list of the world's most valuable brands, published each year in *Business Week* magazine."

-Tom Standage, *A History of the World in 6 Glasses*, 2005

1. a) Explain ONE <u>economic</u> change during the 20th century that is reflected in the passage.

   b) Explain ONE <u>cultural</u> change during the 20th century that is reflected in the passage.

   c) Explain ONE <u>reaction</u> to the economic and cultural change described in the passage above.

Set 6: 1900 to 2001 Primary Source

Use the passages below to answer all parts of the question that follows.

"Workers peasants, soldiers, youth, pupils! Oppressed and exploited compatriots! The Communist Party of Indochina is founded. It is the party of the working class. It will help the proletarian class lead the revolution in order to struggle for all the oppressed and exploited people. From now on we must pin the Party, help it and follow it in order to implement the following slogans:

1. To overthrow French imperialism, feudalism, and the reactionary Vietnamese capitalist class. 2. To make Indochina completely independent. 3. To establish a worker-peasant and soldier government. 4. To confiscate the banks and other enterprises belonging to the imperialists and put them under the control of the worker-peasant and soldier government. 5. To confiscate all of the plantations and property belonging to the imperialists and the Vietnamese reactionary capitalist class and distribute them to poor peasants...."

-Program for Communists of Indochina, Ho Chi Minh (future leader of North Vietnam) for a conference of Vietnamese Communists, 1930.

"Our objective is African union now. There is no time to waste. We must unite now or perish. I am confident that by our concerted effort and determination, we shall lay here the foundations for a continental Union of African States....

On this continent, it has not taken us long to discover that the struggle against colonialism does not end with the attainment of national independence. Independence is only the prelude to a new and more involved struggle for the right to conduct our own economic and social affairs; to construct our society according to our aspirations, unhampered by crushing and humiliating neo-colonialist controls and interference."

-Kwame Nkrumah, President of Ghana, at a meeting in Addis Ababa of 32 African heads of state, 1963.

2. a) Identify ONE common historical process in the 20th century that is reflected in <u>both</u> passages.

b) Explain ONE <u>difference</u> in the goals of Ho Chi Minh and Kwame Nkrumah.

c) Explain ONE <u>reason</u> why Kwame Nkrumah was ultimately unsuccessful in achieving his goal.

Set 6: 1900 to 2001 No Stimulus

Directions: Answer **either** Question 3 **or** Question 4.
Answer all parts of the question that follows.

3. a) Explain ONE economic change in Latin America in the 20th century.

   b) Explain ONE political change in Latin America in the 20th century.

   c) Explain ONE cultural continuity in Latin America in the 20th century.

Answer all parts of the question that follows.

4. a) Explain ONE environmental change in South Asia in the 20th century.

   b) Explain ONE political change in South Asia in the 20th century.

   c) Explain ONE cultural continuity in South Asia in the 20th century.

DOCUMENT-BASED QUESTIONS

DBQ Directions:

There is one document-based question (DBQ) on the exam. It accounts for 25% of your total exam score. This section contains five DBQs in chronological order. The ideal way to use this section is to practice DBQs throughout the year, as you progress through each period of history in class.

In order to prepare for the exam, it is best to replicate exam conditions whenever you practice. For writing DBQs, set a timer for 60 minutes. The College Board has allotted the first 15 of those minutes for document study and the rest for writing, though you are allowed to begin writing before the first 15 minutes are over if you are ready. Write in pen (no whiteout!).

When you are finished, turn to the answer key in the back and read through the annotated student sample essay to see how the essay should be graded. Then use the provided DBQ grading rubric to grade your own!

COMMON MISTAKES (doing any of these will cost you points)	WHAT TO DO INSTEAD
not using all the documents provided	Use all seven documents so that if you accidentally misinterpret a document you are still able to earn full credit for document use.
quoting the document	Use summaries of the relevant parts of the documents. Merely quoting the document does not demonstrate the skill of document interpretation, and therefore does not earn credit as using the document in the essay.
summarizing multiple documents in a single sentence	Summarize documents independently of each other. Each document should have at least one sentence describing it. And always identify specifically which document you are referring to (that's why they are given numbers!).
back-to-back summaries without relating them to the argument	Documents must be used to support an argument. Make sure to explain how the document you summarized relates to the argument you are making.
sourcing a document by only repeating what is in the attribution	Document sourcing must provide information beyond what is already given. You have to use your own knowledge to provide insight into why the document says what it does.

DBQ 1

The document-based question (DBQ) is designed to test your ability to work with and understand historical documents as well as to demonstrate a grasp of historical content and context. In the DBQ essay, you must
- Have a **thesis** that makes a historically defensible claim and responds to all parts of the question.
- Situate your argument by explaining the broader **historical context**, developments and processes.
- Use **topic sentences** that set out a relevant argument using a historical thinking skill.
- Demonstrate a **complex understanding** of the historical development that is the focus of the prompt by using evidence to corroborate, contradict, show cause and effect, show continuity and change over time, qualify (degree), or modify an argument by considering diverse views of evidence (depending on the prompt).
- **Use the documents** to support your arguments. (You should attempt to use all 7 documents; you may omit one, but that is a risk.)
- Explain the significance of the **author's point of view**, the document's historical situation, audience and/or the purpose of at least three documents.
- Refer to **relevant specific historical evidence beyond that found in the documents**. This evidence must be different from evidence used to earn other points on this rubric. A simple mention of evidence is NOT sufficient; you must explain the evidence in the course of your argument. Explaining how the evidence is similar to or different from given information is a good way to earn this point.

Prompt: Evaluate the extent to which increasing interactions among societies during the period 1200 to 1550 contributed to diffusion.

Document 1

> **Friar John of Pian de Carpine, an envoy of Pope Innocent IV to the Mongol Khan, c. 1247.**
>
> We also learnt many private details the [Mongol]Emperor (Güyük Khan) from those who had come with other chiefs, several Ruthenians (Ukrainians) and Hungarians who knew Latin and French, also Ruthenian clerks and others who had been with them, some as long as thirty years, in war and in other events, and who knew all about them as they understood the language, having been continually with them some twenty, others ten years, more or less….
> This Emperor is of medium stature, very prudent and extremely shrewd, and serious and sedate in his manners; and he has never been seen to laugh lightly or show any levity, and of this we were assured by Christians who were constantly with him. We were also assured by Christians who were of his household that they firmly believed that he was about to become a Christian. As signal evidence of this he keeps Christian clerks and gives them allowances, and he has always the chapel of the Christians in front of his great tent, and (these priests) chant publicly and openly and beat (a tablet) according to the fashion of the Greeks at appointed hours, just like other Christians, and though there may be ever so great a multitude of Tartars and of other people. And the other chiefs do not have this.

Document 2

Sugawara Mitsushige, calligrapher who focused on illustrating Japanese Buddhism in the early feudal period, **1257.**

Document 3

Brother John of Monte Corvino, Franciscan friar, from a letter to the Minister General of the Friars Minor in Rome, Yuan China, c. 1280.

I BROTHER JOHN, of Monte Corvino, of the order of Minor Friars, made my way to Cathay (China), the realm of the emperor of the Tartars, who is called the Grand Khan. To him I presented the letter of our lord the Pope and invited him to adopt the Catholic faith of our Lord Jesus Christ; but he had grown too old in idolatry. However, he bestows many kindnesses upon the Christians, and these two years past I am abiding with him. I have built a church in the city of Peking [Beijing], in which the king has his chief residence. This I completed six years ago; and I have built a bell-tower to it and put three bells in it. I have baptized there, as well as I can estimate, up to this time some six thousand persons.
Also, I have gradually bought one hundred and fifty boys, the children of pagan parents, and of ages varying from seven to eleven, who had never learned any religion. These boys I have baptized, and I have taught them Greek and Latin after our manner. … His Majesty the Emperor moreover delights much to hear them chanting. I have the bells rung at all the canonical hours…

Document 4

Ma Tuanlin, Chinese historical writer and encyclopedist, from "A History of the Song," c. 1280.

In this country [Syria] they make gold and silver coins; ten silver coins are worth one gold coin. The inhabitants are just in their dealings, and in the trade, there are not two prices. Cereals are always cheap. When the envoys of neighboring countries arrive at their frontier they are driven by post to the royal capital and, on arrival, are presented with golden money. Their king always wished to send envoys to China; but the Persians wished to carry on trade with them in Han silks, and this is the cause of their having been shut off from direct communication. It was, further, hard to cross the Indian Ocean, travelling merchants taking three years' provisions on board to make this passage, whence the number of travelers was but small. In the beginning of the Yuan-chia period the king of Rome, [Marcus Aurelius Antoninus], sent envoys who offered ivory, rhinoceros' horns, and tortoise-shell, from the boundary of Jih-nan [Annam]; this was the first time they communicated with us. Their tribute contained no precious stones whatever, which fact makes us suspect that the messengers kept them back.

Document 5

The Travels of Marco Polo, **chronicling the merchant Polo's travels through Mongol-controlled Asia, c. 1300.**

It was in the month of November that Kublai returned to Khanbalik [Mongol capital of China]. And there he stayed until February and March, the season of our Easter. Learning that this was one of our principal feasts, he sent for all the Christians and desired them to bring him the book containing the four Gospels. After treating the book to repeated applications of incense with great ceremony, he kissed it devoutly and desired all his barons and lords there present to do the same. This usage he regularly observes on the principle feasts of the Christians, such as Easter and Christmas. And he does likewise on the principle feasts of the Saracens, Jews, and idolaters. Being asked why he did so, he replied: 'There are four prophets who are worshiped and to whom all the world does reverences. The Christians say that their God was Jesus Christ, the Saracens Mahomet, the Jews Moses, and the idolaters Buddha, who was the first to be represented as God in the form of an idol. And I do honor and reverence to all four, so that I may be sure of doing it to him who is greatest in heaven and truest; and to him I pray for aid. But on the Great Khan's own showing he regards as truest and best the faith of the Christians, because he declares that it commands nothing that is not full of all goodness and holiness. He will not on any account allow the Christians to carry the cross before them, and this because on it suffered and died such a great man as Christ.

Document 6

Bar Hebraeus, Bishop of Syria, excerpt from the *Book of the Tower*, 14th century.

The king of the people called Keräit – that is, the Turks who live between the East and the West – lost his way and direction as he found himself caught in a terrible snowstorm while hunting on a great mountain of his land. He was already despairing for his life, when he had the vision of a saint who told him: 'If you believe in Christ, I will lead you out, and you shall not die here'. The king promised he would become a sheep of Christ's fold, and [the saint] guided him and brought him back to a safe way. Having returned to his camp unhurt, [the king] called some Christian traders who lived there and asked them about the [Christian] faith. They told him that [the faith] could not be perfect without baptism. He asked them for a gospel, which he worships every day, and now has sent me a messenger to invite me to go to him in person, or else send a priest to baptize him. He also asks me questions about fasting, explaining: 'My people do not have other nourishment but meat and milk; how, then, could we fast?' And he adds that the number of those who converted to Christianity reaches two hundred thousand.

Document 7

Filofei, a Russian monk, excerpt from a letter to Ivan IV the Terrible, 1530.

I would like to say a few words about the existing Orthodox empire of our most illustrious, exalted ruler. He is the only emperor on all the earth over the Christians, the governor of the holy, divine throne of the holy, ecumenical, apostolic church which in place of the churches of Rome and Constantinople is in the city of Moscow, protected by God, in the holy and glorious Uspenskij Church of the most pure Mother of God. It alone shines over all the earth more radiantly than the sun. For know well, those who love Christ and those who love God, that all Christian empires will perish and give way to the one kingdom of our ruler, in accord with the books of the prophet, which is the Russian empire. For two Romes have fallen, but the third stands, and there will never be a fourth.

DBQ 2

The document-based question (DBQ) is designed to test your ability to work with and understand historical documents as well as to demonstrate a grasp of historical content and context. In the DBQ essay, you must
- Have a **thesis** that makes a historically defensible claim and responds to all parts of the question.
- Situate your argument by explaining the broader **historical context**, developments and processes.
- Use **topic sentences** that set out a relevant argument using a historical thinking skill.
- Demonstrate a **complex understanding** of the historical development that is the focus of the prompt by using evidence to corroborate, contradict, show cause and effect, show continuity and change over time, qualify (degree), or modify an argument by considering diverse views of evidence (depending on the prompt).
- **Use the documents** to support your arguments. (You should attempt to use all 7 documents; you may omit one, but that is a risk.)
- Explain the significance of the **author's point of view**, the document's historical situation, audience and/or the purpose of at least three documents.
- Refer to **relevant specific historical evidence beyond that found in the documents**. This evidence must be different from evidence used to earn other points on this rubric. A simple mention of evidence is NOT sufficient; you must explain the evidence in the course of your argument. Explaining how the evidence is similar to or different from given information is a good way to earn this point.

Prompt: Evaluate the extent that technological developments affected interregional connections between 1400 and 1750.

Document 1

> **Zheng He, admiral of Ming China, c. 1405.**
>
> Under order of the Yongle Emperor I am to set out on a voyage of trade and exploration as the admiral of several fleets. I have spent the past few years building a massive fleet of 317 ships and 28,000 armed crew. We travel to the Indian Ocean and Southeast Asia in order to spread the influence of the Yongle Emperor, and establish control over these maritime trade routes.
>
> - I have admired the great Nine-masted travel ships which I will both travel with and command on our journeys into the unknown. Each one neigh able to hold a quarter of a thousand men. Each crew shall hold more than just merchants and arms-men, but doctors, missionaries, astrologers, cooks, and translators. This fleet of swimming dragons may lead China to great success.

Document 2

Raimondo di Soncino, ambassador of the Duke of Milan in London, from his message to the Duke of Milan, 1497.

My most illustrious and most excellent Lord,

Perhaps amidst so many occupations of your Excellency it will not be unwelcome to learn how the king of England has acquired a part of Asia without drawing his sword. In this kingdom there is a certain Venetian named Zoanne Caboto, of gentle disposition, very expert in navigation, who, seeing that the most serene Kings of Portugal and Spain had occupied unknown islands, meditated the achievement of a similar acquisition for the said Majesty. Having obtained royal privileges … he entrusted his fortune to a small vessel with a crew of 18 persons, and set out from Bristol, a port in the western part of this kingdom. Having passed Ibernia, which is still further to the west, and then shaped a northerly course, he began to navigate to the eastern part, leaving (during several days) the North Star on the right hand; and having wandered thus for a long time, at length he hit upon land, where he hoisted the royal standard, and took possession for his Highness, and, having obtained various proofs of his discovery, he returned. … This Messer Zoanne has the description of the world on a chart, and also on a solid sphere which he has constructed, and on which he shows where he has been…[and] they took so many fish that this kingdom will no longer have need of Iceland, from which country there is an immense trade in the fish they call stock-fish.

Document 3

Girolamo Priuli, a noble of Venice, from his diary, 1501.

This news, as has been said above, was considered very bad news for the city of Venice... Whence it is that the King of Portugal has found this new voyage, and that the spices which were expected which should come from Calicut [Calcutta], Cochin, and other places in India, to Alexandria or Beirut, and later come to Venice, and in this place become monopolized, whence all the world comes to buy such spicery and carry gold, silver, and every other merchandise, with which money the war is sustained; today, with this new voyage by the King of Portugal, all the spices which came by way of Cairo will be controlled in Portugal, because of the caravels which will go to India, to Calicut, and other places to take them. And in this way the Venetians will not be able to take spices either in Alexandria or Beirut.

Document 4

Afonso de Albuquerque, Portuguese sea captain and governor of the State of India, excerpt from his *Memoirs*, 1511.

The king of Portugal has often commanded me to go to the Straits [of Malacca], because...this was the best place to intercept the trade which the Moslems...carry on in these parts. So it was to do Our Lord's service that we were brought here; by taking Malacca, we would close the Straits so that never again would the Moslems be able to bring their spices by this route.... I am very sure that, if this Malacca trade is taken out of their hands, Cairo and Mecca will be completely lost.

Document 5

Martin Waldseemüller, a German cartographer, *Tabula Terre Nove* (*Map of the New Lands*), the first map of the Americas published in an atlas, 1513

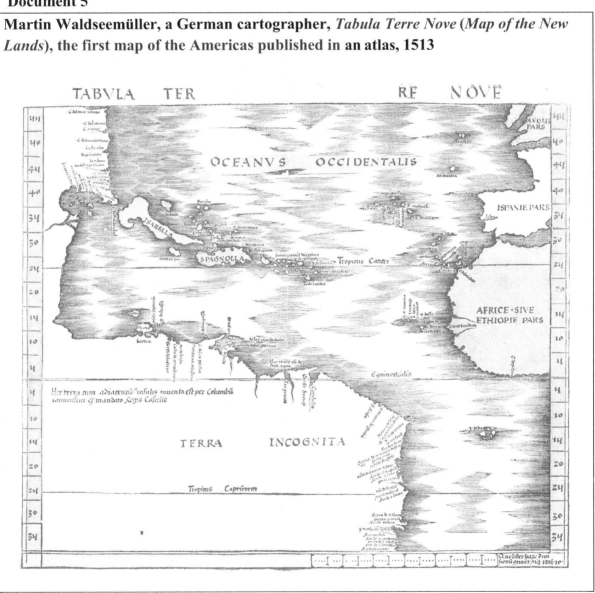

Document 6

A Spanish Carrack – Ferdinand Magellan's ship, the *Victoria*, c. 1510.

Document 7

Marquis Carlos Francisco de Croix, a Spanish general and viceroy of New Spain, from a letter to the Marquis de Henchin, 1769.

"The greater part of the people who each year go from New Spain to the Philippines do not remain there, but return presently, after employing the money which they have.
The failure of the Manila Galleon to arrive causes a scarcity of many things in this country…[the shipment] promises a more brilliant fair at Jalapa, (the town in the *tierra templada* above Vera Cruz). All classes, from the Indians of the torrid lowlands to the Creoles of the capital are dressed in the fabrics of the Far East — the cottons of Luzon or India, or the silks of China.

The Chinese goods form the ordinary dress of the natives of New Spain. The Philippine commerce is acclaimed in this kingdom, because its merchandise supplies the poor folk of the country."

DBQ 3

The document-based question (DBQ) is designed to test your ability to work with and understand historical documents as well as to demonstrate a grasp of historical content and context. In the DBQ essay, you must

- Have a **thesis** that makes a historically defensible claim and responds to all parts of the question.
- Situate your argument by explaining the broader **historical context**, developments and processes.
- Use **topic sentences** that set out a relevant argument using a historical thinking skill.
- Demonstrate a **complex understanding** of the historical development that is the focus of the prompt by using evidence to corroborate, contradict, show cause and effect, show continuity and change over time, qualify (degree), or modify an argument by considering diverse views of evidence (depending on the prompt).
- **Use the documents** to support your arguments. (You should attempt to use all 7 documents; you may omit one, but that is a risk.)
- Explain the significance of the **author's point of view**, the document's historical situation, audience and/or the purpose of at least three documents.
- Refer to **relevant specific historical evidence beyond that found in the documents**. This evidence must be different from evidence used to earn other points on this rubric. A simple mention of evidence is NOT sufficient; you must explain the evidence in the course of your argument. Explaining how the evidence is similar to or different from given information is a good way to earn this point.

Prompt: Evaluate the motives for industrializing powers to establish transoceanic empires in the 19th and early 20th centuries.

Document 1

> **John G. Paton, a British missionary in the Pacific region, a letter to the British government from the New Hebrides Mission, 1883.**
>
> For the following reasons we think the British government ought now to take possession of the New Hebrides group of the South Sea islands, of the Solomon group, and of all the intervening chain of islands from Fiji to New Guinea:
>
> The sympathy of the New Hebrides natives is all with Great Britain, hence they long for British protection, while they fear and hate the French, who appear eager to annex the group, because they have seen the way the French have treated the native races in New Caledonia, the Loyalty Islands, and other South Sea islands.
>
> All the men and all the money used in civilizing and Christianizing the New Hebrides have been British. Now fourteen missionaries and the Dayspring mission ship, and about 150 native evangelists and teachers are employed in the above work on this group…it would be unwise to let any other power now take possession and reap the fruits of all this British outlay.
>
> Because if any other nation takes possession of them, their excellent and spacious harbors, as on Efate, so well-supplied with the best fresh water, and their near-proximity to Great Britain's Australasian colonies, would in time of war make them dangerous to British interests and commerce in the South Seas and her colonies.

Document 2

Jules Ferry, prime minister of France, from a speech before the French Chamber of Deputies, 1884.

Gentlemen, we must speak more loudly and more honestly! We must say openly that indeed the higher races have a right over the lower races ....

I repeat, that the superior races have a right because they have a duty. They have the duty to civilize the inferior races .... In the history of earlier centuries these duties, gentlemen, have often been misunderstood; and certainly, when the Spanish soldiers and explorers introduced slavery into Central America, they did not fulfill their duty as men of a higher race .... But, in our time, I maintain that European nations acquit themselves with generosity, with grandeur, and with sincerity of this superior civilizing duty.

I say that French colonial policy, the policy of colonial expansion, was inspired by... the fact that a navy such as ours cannot do without safe harbors, defenses, supply centers on the high seas .... Are you unaware of this? Look at a map of the world.

At present, as you know, a warship, however perfect its design, cannot carry more than two weeks' supply of coal; and a vessel without coal is a wreck on the high seas. Hence the need to have places of supply, shelters, ports for defense and provisioning....

Document 3

Advertisement from a German newspaper, "Germany Awake!", June 24, 1890.

The diplomacy of the English works swiftly and secretly. What they created burst in the face of the astonished world on June 18th like a bomb---the German-English African Treaty. With one stroke of the pen---the hope of a great German colonial empire was ruined! Shall this treaty really be? No, no and again no! The German people must arise as one and declare that this treaty is unacceptable! . . .The treaty with England harms our interests and wounds our honor; this time it dares not become a reality! We are ready at the call of our Kaiser to step into the ranks and allow ourselves dumbly and obediently to be led against the enemy's shots, but we may also demand in exchange that the reward come to us which is worth the sacrifice, and this reward is: that we shall be a conquering people which takes its portion of the world itself! Deutschland wach auf! [Germany Awake]

Document 4

Wilfred Scawen Blunt, English poet and writer, excerpt from his diaries, 9th Jan. 1896.

… We have now managed in the last six months to quarrel violently with China, Turkey, Belgium, Ashanti, France, Venezuela, America, and Germany. This is a record performance, and if it does not break up the British Empire nothing will. For myself I am glad of it all, for the British Empire is the greatest engine of evil for the weak races now existing in the world---not that we are worse than the French or Italians or Americans---indeed, we are less actively destructive---but we do it over a far wider area and more successfully. I should be delighted to see England stripped of her whole foreign possessions. We are better off and more respected in Queen Elizabeth's time, the "spacious days," when we had not a stick of territory outside the British Islands, than now, and infinitely more respectable. The gangrene of colonial rowdyism is infecting us, and the habit of repressing liberty in weak nations is endangering our own. I should be glad to see the end....

Document 5

Political cartoon from the *Literary Digest* showing U.S. President William McKinley contemplating imperial conquest, 1898.

Document 6

> **John A. Hobson, an English economist and social scientist, excerpt from *Imperialism, A Study*, 1902.**
>
> What is the direct economic outcome of Imperialism? A great expenditure of public money upon ships, guns, military and naval equipment and stores, growing and productive of enormous profits when a war, or an alarm of war, occurs; new public loans and important fluctuations in the home and foreign Bourses; more posts for soldiers and sailors and in the diplomatic and consular services; improvement of foreign investments by the substitution of the British flag for a foreign flag; acquisition of markets for certain classes of exports, and some protection and assistance for trades representing British houses in these manufactures; employment for engineers, missionaries, speculative miners, ranchers and other emigrants.

Document 7

> **Vladimir Illyich Lenin, excerpt from "Imperialism, The Highest Stage of Capitalism," 1916.**
>
> The building of railways seems to be a simple, natural, democratic, cultural and civilizing enterprise; that is what it is in the opinion of bourgeois professors, who are paid to depict capitalist slavery in bright colors, and in the opinion of petty-bourgeois Philistines. But as a matter of fact the capitalist[s]…, have converted this railway construction into an instrument for oppressing a thousand million people (in the colonies and semi colonies), that is, more than half the population of the globe inhabiting the dependent countries, as well as the wage slaves of capital in the "civilized" countries.
>
> Capitalism has grown into a world system of colonial oppression and of the financial strangulation of the overwhelming majority of the population of the world by a handful of "advanced" countries. And this "booty" [spoils] is shared between two or three powerful world marauders armed to the teeth (America, Great Britain, Japan), who involve the whole world in their war over the sharing of their booty.

DBQ 4

The document-based question (DBQ) is designed to test your ability to work with and understand historical documents as well as to demonstrate a grasp of historical content and context. In the DBQ essay, you must

- Have a **thesis** that makes a historically defensible claim and responds to all parts of the question.
- Situate your argument by explaining the broader **historical context**, developments and processes.
- Use **topic sentences** that set out a relevant argument using a historical thinking skill.
- Demonstrate a **complex understanding** of the historical development that is the focus of the prompt by using evidence to corroborate, contradict, show cause and effect, show continuity and change over time, qualify (degree), or modify an argument by considering diverse views of evidence (depending on the prompt).
- **Use the documents** to support your arguments. (You should attempt to use all 7 documents; you may omit one, but that is a risk.)
- Explain the significance of the **author's point of view**, the document's historical situation, audience and/or the purpose of at least three documents.
- Refer to **relevant specific historical evidence beyond that found in the documents**. This evidence must be different from evidence used to earn other points on this rubric. A simple mention of evidence is NOT sufficient; you must explain the evidence in the course of your argument. Explaining how the evidence is similar to or different from given information is a good way to earn this point.

Prompt: To what extent did reactions to the political and social order lead to changes in the 20th century?

Document 1

Belgian colonial official measures the nose to determine whether the man will be classified as Hutu or Tutsi, 1920.

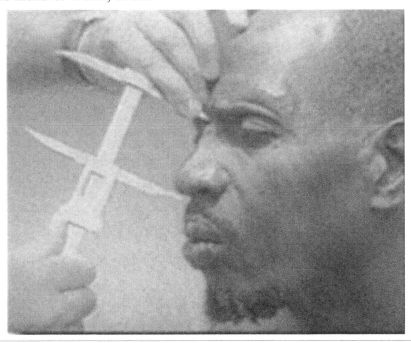

Document 2

Hồ Chí Minh, chairman of the Indochinese Communist Party presented at a mass meeting in Hanoi on September 2, 1945.

Proclamation of Independence of the Democratic Republic of Vietnam

"We hold truths that all men are created equal, that they are endowed by their Creator with certain unalienable Rights, among these are Life, Liberty and the pursuit of Happiness." This immortal statement is extracted from the Declaration of Independence of the United States of America in 1776. Understood in the broader sense, this means: "All peoples on the earth are born equal; every person has the right to live to be happy and free." The Declaration of Human and Civic Rights proclaimed by the French Revolution in 1791 likewise propounds: "Every man is born equal and enjoys free and equal rights." These are undeniable truths. Yet, during and throughout the last eighty years, the French imperialists, abusing the principles of "Freedom, equality and fraternity," have violated the integrity of our ancestral land and oppressed our countrymen. Their deeds run counter to the ideals of humanity and justice.

Document 3

Clement Attlee, British Prime Minister, from a response to requests from President Jinnah of Pakistan for assistance in handling civil disturbances, September 1947.

My colleagues and I have watched with anxiety and deep sympathy the grave developments in India and Pakistan since 15th August and with full understanding of the almost impossible burdens placed on the two new Dominion Governments [India and Pakistan] at the very outset of their career. I am not surprised that, confronted with such a situation, your Government should make an appeal to the United Kingdom Government and other fellow Governments of the Commonwealth....

It is obvious that situation had very nearly got completely out of hand, but there is no doubt in our minds that the Indian Government are doing their utmost to restore order and to prevent violence spreading over still wider areas. Indeed, there appear to be real signs of improvement in the last few days....

It is significant and again no doubt partly due to lack of contact, that the Indian Government appear to have a view of the ability of Pakistan Government to effect pacification hardly less pessimistic than you have of Indian Government.

Document 4

Proclamation of the Algerian National Front, Liberation Front (FLN), November 1954.

After decades of struggle, the National Movement has reached its final phase of fulfilment. At home, the people are united behind the watchwords of independence and action. Abroad, the atmosphere is favorable, especially with the diplomatic support of our Arab and Moslem brothers…Our goal, national independence through the restoration of the Algerian state, (sovereign, democratic, and social), within the framework of the principles of Islam….

The recognition of Algerian nationhood by an official declaration abrogating all edicts, decrees, and laws by virtue of which Algeria was "French soil."

Document 5

Jawaharlal Nehru, India's first Prime Minister. From a speech in Washington, D.C., printed in the *U.S. Department of State Bulletin*, December 1956.

"We are now engaged in a gigantic and exciting task of achieving rapid and large-scale economic development of our country. Such development, in an ancient and underdeveloped country such as India, is only possible with purposive planning… many other countries in Asia tell the same story, for Asia today is resurgent, and these countries which long lay under foreign yoke have won back their independence and are fired by a new spirit and strive toward new ideals. To them, as to us, independence is as vital as the breath they take to sustain life, and colonialism, in any form, or anywhere, is abhorrent…. We think that by the free exchange of ideas and trade and other contacts between nations each will learn from the other and truth will prevail.

Document 6

Kwame Nkrumah, president of Ghana, from the Introduction of *Neo-Colonialism, the Last Stage of imperialism* 1965,

"I propose to analyze neo-colonialism, first, by examining the state of the African continent and showing how neo-colonialism at the moment keeps it artificially poor. Next, I propose to show how in practice African Unity, which in itself can only be established by the defeat of neo-colonialism, could immensely raise African living standards."

Document 7

Hamis Kamuhanda, an 11-year old Tutsi, excerpt from an interview with a BBC reporter, Rwanda, 1994.

The following day we heard rumours that Hutus were out to kill every Tutsi in the country, claiming that we, the Tutsis had killed the Hutu president. We were advised to stay indoors. I had never seen my parents so agitated and terrified all my life. Then there was a knock at the door and before we could even respond, the door fell in and about four or so people came in and dragged my father out by his legs. That was the last we saw of him.

We were hiding under the bed, but we could see everything. Mother told us to keep quiet. Then the shooting began….The bullets came in and hit everything in the way. Yet no-one dared scream. Mother could not cover all four of us.

The armed Hutu men, the Interahamwe, were scattered and patrolling every corner. The situation was tense for a very long time and we could smell the stench of the dead even inside our fenced house. We were terrified. Mother peeped through the wall and saw Tutsi soldiers coming towards the house. She prayed and waited for our fate. What would it be? It was RPF (Rwanda Patriotic Front) soldiers. These were good people. They liberated us and freed us from our self-imposed solitary confinement. The RPF soldiers took me to the hospital. I was there for about six months.

DBQ 5

The document-based question (DBQ) is designed to test your ability to work with and understand historical documents as well as to demonstrate a grasp of historical content and context. In the DBQ essay, you must

- Have a **thesis** that makes a historically defensible claim and responds to all parts of the question.
- Situate your argument by explaining the broader **historical context**, developments and processes.
- Use **topic sentences** that set out a relevant argument using a historical thinking skill.
- Demonstrate a **complex understanding** of the historical development that is the focus of the prompt by using evidence to corroborate, contradict, show cause and effect, show continuity and change over time, qualify (degree), or modify an argument by considering diverse views of evidence (depending on the prompt).
- **Use the documents** to support your arguments. (You should attempt to use all 7 documents; you may omit one, but that is a risk.)
- Explain the significance of the **author's point of view**, the document's historical situation, audience and/or the purpose of at least three documents.
- Refer to **relevant specific historical evidence beyond that found in the documents**. This evidence must be different from evidence used to earn other points on this rubric. A simple mention of evidence is NOT sufficient; you must explain the evidence in the course of your argument. Explaining how the evidence is similar to or different from given information is a good way to earn this point.

Prompt: Evaluate the extent to which government policies sought to affect demography in the 20th century.

Document 1

> **Council of People's Commissars of the USSR,** *Decree on the Prohibition of Abortions*, **June 27, 1936**.
>
> In view of the proven harm of abortions, we forbid the performance of abortions whether in hospitals and special health institutions, or in the homes of doctors and the private homes of pregnant women. ...
> In order to improve the material position of mothers, both working women and employees insured in the organs of social insurance, to increase the allowance issued from the State social insurance funds for the purpose of procuring the necessary articles for infant care, from 32 rubles to 45 rubles.
> To establish a criminal penalty for refusal to employ women for reasons of pregnancy, for reducing their wages on the same grounds…
> To establish a State allowance for mothers of large families: for those having six children, an annual allowance of 2,000 rubles for five years for each subsequent child from the day of its birth, and for mothers having ten children one State allowance of 5,000 rubles on the birth of each subsequent child and an annual allowance of 3,000 rubles for a period of four years following the child's first birthday.

Document 2

Benito Mussolini, Italian Prime Minister, statements made during the 1930s.

Child bearing is women's natural and fundamental mission in life… [Women's work] distracts from reproduction, if it does not directly impede it, and foments independence and the accompanying physical-moral styles contrary to giving birth… Women's place in the present is in the home…Women should be exemplary wives and mothers, guardians of the hearth and subject to the legitimate authority of the husband... The fate of nations is intimately bound up with their powers of reproduction. All nations and all empires first felt decadence gnawing at them when their birth rate fell off.

Document 3

Adolf Hitler, German chancellor, part of a speech made to the Nazi Women's League, 1934.

The sacrifices which the man makes in the struggle of his nation, the woman makes in the preservation of that nation in individual cases. What the man gives in courage on the battlefield, the woman gives in eternal self-sacrifice, in eternal pain and suffering. Every child that a woman brings into the world is a battle, a battle waged for the existence of her people. And both must therefore mutually value and respect each other when they see that each performs the task that Nature and Providence have ordained. And this mutual respect will necessarily result from this separation of the functions of each.

Whereas previously the programs of the liberal, intellectualist women's movements contained many points, the program of our National Socialist women's movement has but one single point, and that point is the child, that tiny creature which must be born and grow strong and which alone gives meaning to the whole life-struggle.

Document 4

Fidel Castro, Prime Minister of Cuba, part of the *Working Woman Maternity Law*, signed at the Palace of the Revolution, in Havana, 1974.

The law protects the working woman's maternity, guaranteeing and facilitating her medical attention during pregnancy, her rest before and after delivery, the breastfeeding and care of the children as well as a financial aid in some cases. …

Every pregnant working woman, regardless of type of work will be obliged to stop working on the 34th week of pregnancy, and will have the right to a leave of absence of 18 weeks…

If the working woman, because of complications during delivery, requires a longer period of recovery beyond the postnatal leave, she will have the right to receive the subsidy for illness as established in the Social Security Law. …

The financial aid that the working woman will receive during her maternity leave will be equal to the weekly average of salaries and subsidies she has received during the twelve months immediately prior to the leave. This aid will never be under ten pesos a week. …

In order to guarantee the care and development of the child during his first year of life, the working women will have the right every month to one day off, with pay, to take her child for a pediatric check-up.

Document 5

Excerpt from the *Union Territory of Delhi Administration*, India, 1975.

For the General Public

Only individuals who have been able to show by their ration cards that they have two or less than two children will be allowed free medical coverage in Government hospitals. Those having more than two children will receive this free coverage only after producing a sterilization certificate from the authority prescribed in respect of the husband.

Document 6

Central Committee of the Communist Party of China, an open letter to all members of the Communist Youth League, 1980.

Communist Party members and Communist Youth League comrades across the country:

In order to fight for the control of China's total population within 1.2 billion by the end of this century, the State Council has issued a call to the people of the whole country to promote the birth of only one child to a couple. This is a major measure that relates to the speed and future of the four modernization drives, the health and happiness of future generations, and the long-term interests and current interests of the people of the country…

In the 30 years since the founding of the People's Republic of China, a population of more than 600 million people was born…The population has grown so fast that people across the country are experiencing greater difficulties in eating, dressing, housing, transportation, education, health, employment, etc., making it difficult for the entire country to change poverty and backwardness in a short period of time.

Document 7

National Population Policies, report published by the United Nations, 2001.

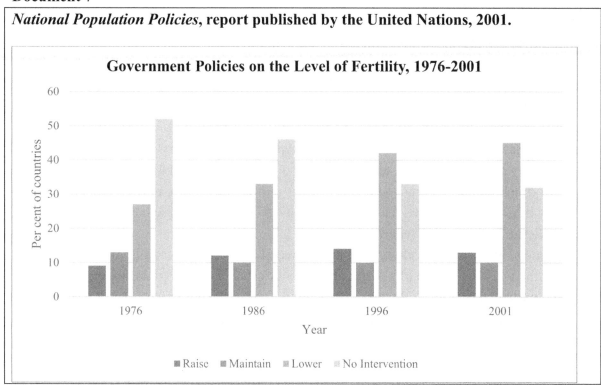

LONG ESSAY QUESTIONS

LEQ Directions:

The long essay question (LEQ) accounts for 15% of your total exam score. In the exam, you will be given the option of three different prompts to choose from, all of which will be written in the same style but will cover different time periods. This section includes four sets of three questions that can be answered with any of the course's historical thinking skills—causation, comparison, and continuity and change over time. The ideal way to use this section is to practice the LEQs in chronological order throughout the year, as you progress through each period of history in class.

In order to prepare for the exam, it is best to replicate exam conditions whenever you practice. For writing LEQs, pick a prompt to respond to and set a timer for 40 minutes. Write in pen (no whiteout!).

When you are finished, turn to the answer key in the back and read through the scoring guide for your prompt. Then use the provided LEQ grading rubric to grade your own!

COMMON MISTAKES (doing any of these will cost you points)	WHAT TO DO INSTEAD
writing off-topic	Carefully read the prompt several times before you begin. Write a thesis statement that uses the key words and has at least two historically defensible arguments (three is preferred) in it. Then, use the key words from the prompt frequently throughout your essay to ensure that you stay on topic and answer the question.
using vague statements or generalities as evidence	Be as precise and specific as you can when writing about a topic. Writing generally about a topic might help develop your argument, but it will not provide the information that earns you up to two points for evidence. Proper nouns are your friend.
not demonstrating the tested skill	-For *Causation*, make sure to differentiate between causes and effects. If you can add nuance to your argument, such as explaining which cause was most important, or explaining which effects were short-term and which were long-term, you are setting yourself up to earn the complexity point. -For *Comparison*, the differences are the most complicated to explain. Use "degree" to qualify a difference, using words like "more," "less," "larger," smaller," etc. -For *Continuity and Change Over Time*, identify a "pivotal moment" which spurred on the changes. You need to explain why the changes occurred, and the pivotal movement makes it much easier. -NOTE: some prompts are worded in such a way that you could use more than one skill to answer them. If that is the case, pick ONE skill to demonstrate in your thesis. You can always use the other skills, but they should come secondary and simply provide additional explanation for your larger argument.

LEQ 1

Directions: Choose EITHER question A, question B, or question C.

In your response you should do the following:

• Respond to the prompt with a historically defensible thesis or claim that establishes a line of reasoning.
• Describe a broader historical context relevant to the prompt.
• Support an argument in response to the prompt using specific and relevant examples of evidence.
• Use historical reasoning (e.g., comparison, causation, continuity or change over time) to frame or structure an argument that addresses the prompt.
• Use evidence to corroborate, qualify, or modify an argument that addresses the prompt.

A. In the period 1200 to 1450, belief systems and their practices influenced society.

   Develop an argument that evaluates the extent to which belief systems and their practices influenced social structures in one or more societies during this period.

B. In the period between 1450 to 1750 belief systems underwent significant changes.

   Develop an argument that evaluates the extent to which changes to belief systems caused political, cultural, or social implications in one or more regions during this period.

C. In the period 1750 to 1900 industrialization caused changes to existing social hierarchies.

   Develop an argument that evaluates the extent to which industrialization influenced social structures in one or more regions during this period.

LEQ 2

Directions: Choose EITHER question A, question B, or question C.

In your response you should do the following:

• Respond to the prompt with a historically defensible thesis or claim that establishes a line of reasoning.
• Describe a broader historical context relevant to the prompt.
• Support an argument in response to the prompt using specific and relevant examples of evidence.
• Use historical reasoning (e.g., comparison, causation, continuity or change over time) to frame or structure an argument that addresses the prompt.
• Use evidence to corroborate, qualify, or modify an argument that addresses the prompt.

A. Between 1200 and 1450 the expansion of empires influenced trade and communication.

   Develop an argument that evaluates the extent to which expanding empires affected trade in one or more regions during this period.

B. Between 1450 and 1750 there were changes to the networks of exchange.

   Develop an argument that evaluates the extent to which changes to the networks of exchange affected societies in one or more regions during this period.

C. The global economy experienced change after 1900.

   Develop an argument that evaluates the extent to which economic processes changed society in one or more regions during this period.

LEQ 3

Directions: Choose EITHER question A, question B, or question C.

In your response you should do the following:

• Respond to the prompt with a historically defensible thesis or claim that establishes a line of reasoning.
• Describe a broader historical context relevant to the prompt.
• Support an argument in response to the prompt using specific and relevant examples of evidence.
• Use historical reasoning (e.g., comparison, causation, continuity or change over time) to frame or structure an argument that addresses the prompt.
• Use evidence to corroborate, qualify, or modify an argument that addresses the prompt.

A. Between 1200 and 1450 a variety of internal and external factors contributed to state formation.

   Develop an argument that evaluates how states gained and maintained power in one or more regions during this period.

B. Between 1450 and 1750 various land-based empires developed and expanded.

   Develop an argument that evaluates how empires gained and maintained power in one or more regions during this period.

C. In the period 1750 to 1900 state power shifted in various parts of the world.

   Develop an argument that evaluates how state power shifted in one or more regions during this period.

LEQ 4

Directions: Choose EITHER question A, question B, or question C.

In your response you should do the following:

• Respond to the prompt with a historically defensible thesis or claim that establishes a line of reasoning.
• Describe a broader historical context relevant to the prompt.
• Support an argument in response to the prompt using specific and relevant examples of evidence.
• Use historical reasoning (e.g., comparison, causation, continuity or change over time) to frame or structure an argument that addresses the prompt.
• Use evidence to corroborate, qualify, or modify an argument that addresses the prompt.

A. Between 1200 and 1450 networks of exchange resulted in environmental changes in Afro-Eurasia.

Develop an argument that evaluates the environmental effects of the networks of exchange in one or more regions during this period.

B. In the period 1450 to 1750 the Columbian exchange affected the Eastern and Western Hemispheres.

Develop an argument that evaluates the environmental effects of the Columbian Exchange in one or more regions during this period.

C. In the period 1900 to the present human activity affected the environment in significant ways.

Develop an argument that evaluates how human activity affected the environment in one or more regions during this period.

ANSWER KEY

MC Test 1 : 1200 to 1600

Questions 1-3 refer to Topic 1.1

1. **(B)** The passage describes the Song rulers as relying on the "thousand-year-old traditions" of the "Confucian state," clearly indicating the importance of tradition. It also explains how their insistence on valuing scholarship as the ideal went beyond previous dynasties, meaning that their government was not identical to previous dynasties. There is no mention of nomadic invasions in the passage.

2. **(C)** The Song dynasty is perhaps most remembered for its cultural vibrancy. Many of the cultural characteristics often associated with China originated in the Song dynasty. Song culture spread along trade routes and influenced neighboring regions. Buddhism remained a strong influence in the arts and in Neoconfucianism. The other two choices are not cultural effects and are factually incorrect as well: the conditions of the peasant class remained largely the same as it had been in previous eras, and the Confucian-based civil service exam remained in use.

3. **(D)** The Song government valued scholar-officials over those with military experience resulting in in military weakness, making them vulnerable to attacks from nomadic groups on their borders. Their territory grew smaller, not larger, and they were eventually conquered by the Mongols. Contact with Japan and epidemic diseases did not bring about political change in China at this time.

Questions 4-6 refer to Topic 1.2

4. **(C)** The image shows what seem to be scholars engaged in discussion surrounded by stacks of books in a library. This suggests a rich intellectual tradition (especially compared to Western Europe in the 13th century, where books were rare). It does not by itself suggest that everyone in the society could read, nor does it give any clear insight into the literacy of women. It is unclear whether the books were printed on paper or animal skin.

5. **(A)** Islam was strongly influenced by the religions that already existed in the Arabian Peninsula, including Christianity and Judaism (they share common holy texts), and Zoroastrianism (they share a dualistic view of morality and the afterlife). Christians were a minority in the region and were not politically dominant. Hinduism and Buddhism have few adherents in the region and therefore did not influence Islam's formation. Initially Islam was a fairly egalitarian religion, based on the social traditions of the Arab pastoralists.

6. **(D)** Muslim rule expanded because of military expansion, merchant and missionary activity, and the *weakening* of the Byzantine empire. The question asks which was NOT a reason why Muslim rule expanded, so the correct answer is the *growth* of Byzantine power.

Questions 7-9 refer to Topic 1.1

7. **(B)** Though some technology is visible in the painting, there is not enough to definitively prove China was so advanced. The painting works better as proof of a thriving urban culture in China, with its dense crowds, bustling streets, and large, ornate buildings. The painting does not reveal anything regarding China's political state or social hierarchies (which was not in any way egalitarian until the 20th century).

8. **(D)** While China's relatively isolated geographic location did help protect it from potential political rivals to its west, China's economy flourished during the Song dynasty due to trade—both regional and long-distance. The Song were producing huge quantities of manufactured goods, such as porcelain, and shipping them along expanded land and sea trading routes. Though China had large cities at the time, the peasant class remained largely rural and agricultural. Nomads did play a key role in the transfer of knowledge, but those who gained the most from it were in the west.

9. **(A)** Europe was broken up into relatively small, feudal kingdoms at the time, much less centralized than China. China was more urbanized than Europe, with some cities reaching populations of over 100,000 people. Both societies remained staunchly patriarchal. The increased demand for luxury goods largely benefited China's economy, as luxury goods were their main export, flowing from East to West along the Silk Roads.

Question 10-12 refer to Topic 2.3

10. **(C)** By the 1200s, sailing technology had become more advanced since the time when the sail was first introduced in Ancient Egypt. The Portuguese and Spanish would not have major breakthroughs in navigational technology until the 15th century. The use of slave labor in the Indian Ocean region did not contribute to naval technology.

11. **(D)** Trade and travel throughout the Indian Ocean region increased between 1200 and 1450 because of a greater understanding of the monsoon wind patterns and currents. Mongol control actually made overland travel safer (though once their reign collapsed, overland travel became much more dangerous again). Muslim pilgrims to Mecca took advantage of the already existing networks and did not build their own. The Dutch and British would not be involved in Indian Ocean trade until the 1500s.

12. **(B)** Increased trade led to new, larger, and wealthier trading cities developing in the Indian Ocean region. Islam became a powerful force in the region, as most of the sailing traders were Muslim Arabs. Hinduism didn't spread to East Africa until the 19th century due to labor migrations within the British Empire (the British government did not take direct control of Indian until 1858).

Questions 13-15 refer to Topic 2.2

13. **(D)** In the passage, Guyuk states that the Mongol's success in conquering so much Christian territory is evidence that God approves what they are doing and blesses them. It seems that he most likely wrote this letter to intimidate the Pope, not out of interest in and respect for Christianity.

14. **(B)** The passage describes Mongol women as being incredibly capable, with skills and roles similar to those of men. It is apparent from the passage that women are highly valued in the society; this attitude differs from most other Asian cultures at the time (especially in China and India).

15. **(B)** The use of horse-related technology made the Mongol army an incredibly mobile and deadly force. Their use of stirrups allowed them to maintain speed on horseback while using both hands to stabilize and aim their bow. Saddles were also crucial to their success, as they enabled the Mongols to ride for hours on end over vast distances (they did not travel by foot).

Questions 16-18 refer to Topic 1.2

16. **(C)** The depiction of an Islamic hospital illustrates that Muslim doctors had knowledge of the benefits of quarantining the sick as early as the 9th century. This shows that they were not entirely superstitious about the spread of disease. They were much more advanced in medicine than Europe at the time. Nothing in the illustration references the commonly held idea of the "four bodily humors" determining a person's health.

17. **(B)** In the passage it is stated that hospitals should treat everyone, despite their social status, without payment. This is in line with Muhammad's teachings, as one of the tenets of Islam is charity. Just because the hospital treats both men and women does not make them equal or indicate that there was no social hierarchy. The passage says nothing about how education affects social mobility.

18. **(D)** The illustration of al-Razi was done by a European who was translating Arabic texts, which is evidence of Islamic cultural diffusion into Europe. This cultural diffusion occurred in part because of the increased interactions of the two groups during the Crusades. All the other options are untrue.

Questions 19-22 refer to Topic 2.2

19. **(A)** Paper currency made trade easier because it could be used in the same way metal coins were, but was easier to carry in large amounts. As opportunities for trade increased, the use of paper currency became the preferred method. Paper currency did not reduce theft. Paper currency's value was not based on the value of paper as a good in the same way metal coins were. Paper currency was backed by gold and silver—it was not created due to a shortage of gold and silver.

20. **(C)** Checking (where a person in one country could cash a check drawn on his bank in another country) was introduced during the Abbasid dynasty. The barter system and standardized coin weights both existed since before the Common Era. Double entry accounting was first used among Jewish communities in the Middle East during the 11th century before making its way to Europe.

21. **(A)** Marco Polo was a traveling merchant from Venice who wrote about what he encountered along Eurasian trade routes. Paper currency was a Chinese innovation, and Marco Polo was one of the first who exposed Europeans to the concept. His description of paper currency is not spreading belief systems, nor is he engaging in trading luxury goods. His travels and writings were something he did independently, not as a spy.

22. **(B)** The images show that the Mongols (who founded the Yuan Dynasty) adopted the system of paper currency from the Chinese. From the images provided, no judgement can be made regarding European printing at the time. There is also nothing to provide information about the ease of forgery or the success of different groups of merchants.

Questions 23-26 refer to Topic 2.7

23. **(B)** From what is provided in the passage, the two groups seem get along peacefully and benefit from their interactions. There is no evidence of Europeans in the passage. There is no evidence of war or of an alliance.

24. **(C)** The passage notes that the king's daughters entered into arranged marriages set up by their father. There is no mention of what women's rights are *within* the marriage. There is no indication of the status of merchants in regards to farmers and religious leaders.

25. **(D)** Both East and West Africa were known for their gold, not for semi-precious stones. There is no indication that Africans wanted spice and silk. Muslim traders did not use cheap African labor for textile production.

26. **(B)** Conversion to Islam was often more of an individual choice for Africans than conversion to Christianity for Native Americans, who were frequently threatened with violence if they did not convert. Both religions became the dominant religion in their respective areas, and both religions led to restrictions on women's rights (especially Christianity).

Questions 27-29 refer to Topic 2.7

27. **(D)** The diagram shows that the Chinese ship is much larger and more complex than the European ship. It shows nothing in regard to the size of the regions' forests or the wealth of the ships' captains. The large size of the Chinese ship does not necessarily mean they had a greater need of foreign goods (they didn't; they were self-sufficient).

28. **(C)** The Ming government sponsored Zheng He's voyages for the purpose of spreading Chinese prestige and influence. Though Zheng He did travel to Africa, there is no real evidence that he made it around the Cape of Good Hope. Zheng He's voyages were largely successful—pirates were subdued and tribute was accepted. The voyages ended when Zheng He died and the Chinese found new voyages to be too expensive.

29. **(C)** The Ming government wanted Vietnam and others to make tribute payments. The Americas were unknown to China at this time and Europe's naval power had not yet become a threat. While the Ming were interested in any threats in the Indian Ocean, they were not interested in controlling trade.

Questions 30-32 refer to Topics 2.3 and 2.5

30. **(C)** In the passage, Ibn Battuta explicitly states that he left Tangier "with the intention of making the Pilgrimage to the Holy House and the Tomb of the Prophet." He is referring to the *hajj* to Mecca which is a requirement for all able-bodied Muslims. Nowhere in the passage does it mention that he is going for financial of diplomatic reasons.

31. **(C)** Coastal towns link the interior with sea routes, making them hubs, or "entrepots," of long-distance trade. Because of all the merchant activity, these towns become quite prosperous and well-regarded. There is no evidence to suggest they were exporting large amounts of meat and fruit—the passage says they are eating these items themselves.

32. **(D)** All three left written records. None of them were looking for a "new" route, but were traveling along established trade routes. None had the goal of spreading religion, and only Zheng He was government-sponsored.

Questions 33-35 refer to Topic 1.6

33. **(C)** The key words of the question are "according to Boccaccio," and Boccaccio writes in the passage that the plague was sent "by the just anger of God." There was indeed a poor understanding of how diseases were transmitted in the 14th century, but Boccaccio does not mention it. Nor does he mention Italy's isolation from the rest of Europe (which is false) or the plague traveling from the Americas (which is also false.)

34. **(A)** The plague was transmitted due to long-distance trade from Central Asia to Western Europe, which had increased due to the relative safety of the Silk Roads under Mongol rule. The plague did not originate along the routes of the Hanseatic league. There was no such thing as the "Italian Empire," and the commercial growth of Florence alone was not enough to spark the kind of trade needed for the plague to spread.

35. **(B)** With the death of a large part of the population, the feudal system broke down as labors demanded wages and many moved to the growing urban areas. The Catholic Church actually lost power as it could not provide an adequate explanation of what happened. Women's status remained generally unchanged in the long-term, and the Renaissance is not connected to the plague, but rather to an increase in wealth due to trade.

Questions 36-39 refer to Topic 4.2

36. **(C)** Columbus makes it very clear that during the reign of Ferdinand and Isabella the only acceptable faith in Spain was Christianity. He denigrates both the Muslims and the Jews – groups that suffered immensely in this period of the Inquisition and the *Reconquista*. The Spanish monarchs had no desire to make a cultural pact with India.

37. **(C)** Although Columbus was also driven by a desire for fame and the promise of financial reward, in the first paragraph he stresses his devoutness to the Catholic faith and is determined to proselytize Christianity. He had no idea that he would end up in the Americas.

38. **(B)** The voyages of Columbus inspired other mariners to try their luck and effectively led to the period known as the Voyages of Exploration. It was primarily the Portuguese that introduced the most important European technology in this era. The Spanish concentrated on sending expedition to the Middle Americas, and it was the British and French who sailed the North Atlantic. Although American foods did become staples in other regions it was a long-term, not short-term, consequence.

39. **(D)** Although there was formerly a tendency to among Western historians to celebrate the voyages of Columbus, a new revisionist approach to history tends to accept that the negative consequences are also very important.

Questions 40-41 refer to Topic 1.4

40. **(A)** The Nahuatl language of the Aztecs was traditionally written using hieroglyphics, but in the image a script using the Latin alphabet is used instead. This is evidence of the diffusion of Spanish culture in the Americas. There is no sign of Christianity, disease, or European technology in the illustration.

41. **(D)** The different groups of people depicted in the image are shown in an organized way, in different sizes (most likely based on rank in society), and in different styles of dress. This illustrates that Aztec society was diverse and highly organized (not "primitive"). The illustration, through depicting the level of importance of different groups, makes clear that Aztec society was not egalitarian. The image doesn't reveal anything about the role of women in public life.

Questions 42-44 refer to Topic 2.4

42. **(B)** Leo Africanus focuses a great deal on the market activity that he witnessed, providing evidence of a strong economy based on trade. Timbuktu was not isolated despite its desert location as it was on important trade routes. The passage mentions other goods besides textiles that are traded there, such as agricultural goods and salt.

43. **(C)** With more trade across the Sahara, more African goods, especially gold, found their way into the Eurasian market. Despite the introduction of Islam, gender structure did not change significantly until the coming of Europeans and Atlantic slavery. There was no important change to the African environment at this time, and trading centers were not hubs for West African merchants.

44. **(A)** The arrival of the Portuguese along the west coast of Africa brought great change as the economies of the two regions became intertwined. Inter-regional African trade continued to be conducted by African traders. Mercantilism was a policy that occurred later as Europeans sought to colonize large parts of the world. African foods were not widely spread until they were taken aboard ships carrying slaves to the Americas.

Questions 45-46 refer to Topics 3.2 and 3.3

45. **(D)** The elaborate clothes of the rulers and the sumptuous furnishings were designed to impress the subjects and foreign emissaries. While the Safavids did have a patriarchal society and an unequal society, this is not clearly shown in the image. Also, despite the strength of the Safavid military, it is not the focus of this painting.

46. **(C)** The main difference between the Safavids and the Ottomans was the difference in which Islamic sect was dominant. By this era, the split between Sunnis and Shiites was wide and violent. The Shiite Safavid Empire was rich and fought the Sunni Ottomans for ideological and territorial reasons.

Questions 47-49 refer to Topic 3.3

47. **(B)** Generations of prosperity had allowed the Chinese government (not private merchants) to take on large infrastructure projects, most notably the Grand Canal. Water transportation was a priority mainly to transport goods, not for military purposes, as China rarely had large military conflicts with her neighbors. Water transportation was preferred not because it was safer, but because it was faster.

48. **(C)** China had a near monopoly on the tea trade. Europeans (especially the British), once they had access to it, became heavy consumers of tea. China was not the only region of the world suitable to grow tea, and tea was later grown all over the world. There was no such belief among Medieval doctors that imbibing hot fluids was harmful, and even if there was, the European market did not dominate global trade at this time.

49. **(B)** The Jesuits were in China in an effort to convert as many people as possible to Catholicism (they were going on missions to the Americas at this time as well). The Jesuits were not trying to create a new religion. They were not part of the military, and they were also not seeking trade agreements.

Questions 50-53 refer to Topics 3.2 and 3.3

50. **(A)** Intensification of trade and resulting economic prosperity best explains the abundance and diversity of goods mentioned in the first source. The places where the clothing is made are referred to as "imperial workshops," meaning they were under government control. There is no mention in the passage of from where the textiles are sourced.

51. **(C)** Akbar created Dīn-i Ilāhī, or the "divine faith," which combined aspects from all the religions (particularly Hinduism and Islam) in his diverse empire. Though very few people actually converted, it was a way for Akbar to officially avoid any tension and resentment that would arise from favoring one religious group over another.

52. **(D)** The second source describes a prosperous economy that produces luxury goods on a large scale through the work of highly-skilled artisans. This kind of production is only possible if there is a lot of trade. There is no mention that this type of production is new to India, and it does not indicate where in India this production was taking place.

53. **(B)** The second source indicates that people remain in the social position in which they are born, and that professions are passed down from parent to child. This suggests a rigid caste system. There is no mention of women's status, of family size, or the middle class.

Questions 54-55 refer to Topic 3.1

54. **(A)** The Turkish emperor is declaring war by making outrageous demands of the Germans that he knows they will not meet (that they must convert to Islam). While operating under the guise of religion, his main goal is to conquer more territory for his empire. Though there are likely economic motives for this, the passage does not mention any, nor does it mention using the Germans as slaves.

55. **(B)** He is taking advantage of Germany's (and Europe's) weakness as the Thirty Years' War had devastated Europe's population and weakened its armies. The Thirty Years' War begun partly due to religious rivalries that formed between different groups of Christians after the Reformation. The Black Death and the decline of the Silk Roads had both happened centuries before. At this point in time, the Turks no longer had any major technological advantage over European armies.

MC Test 2 : 1200 to 2001

Questions 1-3 refer to Topic 2.2

1. **(C)** The second paragraph describes the various steps involved with making and issuing currency. While there is mention of both paper and silk worms, the passage is not about book-making or silk. There is no mention of alchemy, either.

2. **(B)** According to the first paragraph, war harnesses and other nomadic warfare technology were displayed in fine palaces along the city wall. There is no mention of Polo himself, other Chinese cities, or Confucian philosophy.

3. **(C)** The excerpt describes production of paper currency, which supports trade by addressing the limitations of coinage, namely difficult production and transportation. Although there is mention of the Byzantines, the excerpt is not about trade on the Silk Road. Government involvement in the economy is explicitly described, and there is no indication of a free enterprise economy is the passage. There is not enough evidence that Polo was "intimately" aware of economics, he simply knew how they produced their paper currency.

Questions 4-6 refer to Topic 2.2

4. **(B)** Though he admits that the Khan is not interested in converting to Christianity, Corvina spends most of the passage detailing how successful he has been converting the Mongols to Christianity. He does not explicitly ask for more priests, though he does offer information on the safest route East.

5. **(C)** The eastward spread of Christianity is a cultural transfer that was largely due to the expansion of the Mongol's political control via contact with (and violent conquest of) other states. While trading centers did increase, it is relevant to the passage. The Reformation did not occur until 200 years after this passage was written.

6. **(A)** As the Mongols dominated a large swatch of Eurasia, they spurred on travel, communication, and trade through protecting trade routes. They did not expect others to convert to their religion as it was closely tied to their specific geographic origins. Though some Mongols settled in cities, most maintained their nomadic lifestyle. No lasting political alliances came out of resistance to Mongol invasion.

Questions 7-9 refer to Topic 1.6

7. **(C)** The illustration depicts technology that enabled Europeans to cultivate the heavy soil of the Northern European Plain. Although wheat was an important crop in France, it is not the subject of the illustration. Using the three-field rotation, a field was left fallow every three years, and laborers lived in villages at the center of their lord's manor.

8. **(C)** Castles were built for protection (not for tourists) and offered protection to the serfs and were used as a safe haven during the period when Europe was plagued by lawlessness and invasions. Although the church was very powerful in this feudal period, there was no power struggle between the church and the lords. Fairs usually took place in towns and cities, not in castles.

9. **(B)** In the feudal period in Western Europe, the main labor system was that of serfdom as peasants gave their labor in return for protection. Plantation labor did not exist in Western Europe, and mining was less important than agriculture.

Questions 10-13 refer to Topic 4.2

10. **(C)** The map would be most useful showing the explorations of Christopher Columbus to the Caribbean, as they occurred before the map was made in 1502. Ferdinand Magellan's circumnavigation of the globe and the Portuguese arrival at Tanegashima both occurred after the map was already made. The map is unlikely to show the voyages of Zheng He as the European cartographer most likely had no knowledge of them.

11. **(B)** The astrolabe was used for calculating latitude, and had recently be reintroduced to Europeans by Arab sailors. Polo's journal did not have accurate measurements, while Galileo's calculations would not have helped with a nautical chart. The compass does not measure latitude.

12. **(B)** Europeans finding a direct route to India meant they could bypass Ottoman traders, which ultimately weakened Muslim control of trade from Asia. The Portuguese did not come to politically dominate India, only some coastal trading ports. If anything, the easier access heightened the demand of Europeans for Asian goods by making them more accessible. The Ming Dynasty was not affected by European involvement in Indian Ocean trade.

13. **(C)** The primary reason for 15th and 16th century voyages of exploration was economic in nature. The Europeans wanted mostly to avoid, not to weaken, Muslim control of trade from Asia. Discovering barbarian people and even proselytizing the Christian faith was secondary to the ultimate goal of gaining wealth.

Questions 14-15 refer to Topic 4.3

14. **(A)** The new connections between the Eastern and Western Hemispheres resulted in the exchange of new plants, animals, and diseases, known as the Columbian Exchange. African crops were never popular in Europe, and food was grown locally and not imported. The tomato cannot be considered a luxury good and the impact of its arrival from the Americas took many years.

15. **(C)** The potato, another American plant, provided cheap, nutritious, and ample sustenance for people in both Europe and Asia. Famine continued to haunt many regions, and still does to this day. The potato never replaced the staples of Africa—yams, sorghum, and millet.

Questions 16-18 refer to Topics 3.1 and 3.2

16. **(D)** The passage explicitly states that men rise in service based on merit, and also mentions that Christians and Jews are protected and therefore tolerated. The passage does not mention women or special treatment of foreigners.

17. **(B)** *Devshirme* was a system created in order to fill positions in the military and bureaucracy with men trained from childhood. Though they could be bureaucrats, they were not intended for the sole purpose of acting as translators. Women were not part of the *devshirme* system. The Ottoman Empire did not control India—that was the Mughal Empire.

18. **(D)** European kings' construction of palaces like Versailles was a way to legitimize and consolidate power as a display of grandeur, wealth, and control of resources. The Safavid Empire did not use human sacrifice, that was the Aztecs. The Mughals did not use an exam system, that was the Chinese. Chinese emperors actually cracked down on Christianity during this time period.

Questions 19-21 refer to Topics 3.1, 3.2, and 3.4

19. **(C)** Peter was dealing with the problem that Russia was not taken seriously by powerful European countries, largely due to cultural differences. Peter had control over the Orthodox church to a great degree. The passage does not address disparities between social classes. While healthcare is always an issue, there is no mention of it in the passage, and Russia's population was not aging.

20. **(D)** The Ottoman Empire, or "Turkish Empire," as mentioned in the prompt, was a threat to Russia's southern border, as Peter desired a warm-water port on the Black Sea. The fact that Russia was at war constantly during Peter's reign is not necessarily a problem, and therefore, while true, is not the best answer choice. Russia was seen as backward, but not shunned by other European nations. Russia was not threated by the Qing as it did not have full control over northern Asia at the time.

21. **(C)** Russia's interactions and interests in the West at this time did not alter the fundamental agricultural characteristics of Russia, as there was no industrialization at this time. The Russian Orthodox culture remained stable, and the peasant class remained unaltered until the end of serfdom in the late 1800s.

Questions 22-24 refer to Topic 6.2

22. **(C)** Emperor Joseph II grants the serfs of Austria the right to leave their manor and take a different job. He is not granting them equal rights as landowners—they still have to request permits from the lord of the manor. He is not giving them permission to rebel, and he is not granting them the right to have serfs of their own—he is ending serfdom.

23. **(B)** Religious toleration was a major idea that came out of the Enlightenment, and is the best answer. Capitalism, not mercantilism, was a product of the Enlightenment. Monumental architecture is not especially enlightened or unenlightened; the same with colonialism.

24. **(D)** Catherine II of Russia was encouraged by Voltaire to end serfdom, but never did. Serfdom had ended in Britain long before George III of Britain took the throne. Louis XVI actually did end the last vestiges of serfdom before he was beheaded. Mehmet's Ottoman Empire did not have a system of serfdom.

Questions 25-27 refer to Topic 5.2

25. **(C)** Sieyès is demanding political power for the Third Estate, which was comprised of everyone who was not part of the clergy or the aristocracy, but was not given proportional representation in the French government. He is not trying to gain support for King Louis XVI or the Catholic Church. Nor is he concerned about immigrants.

26. **(B)** The immediate result of the agreement signed at Versailles was the storming of the Bastille fortress by angry Parisians who wanted to secure weapons for the troubles ahead. The executions by guillotine, the attack on the Catholic Church, and the rise of Napoleon all came later in the revolution.

27. **(D)** Between publication of the two passages, the Third Estate demanded an equal vote when the Estates General met at Versailles. The other events all took place after the Tennis Court Oath, which is the subject of the second passage.

Questions 28-29 refer to Topic 5.2

28. **(B)** The grotesque portrayal of the French *sans-culottes* is clearly meant to turn British citizens against the French Revolution. The *Modest Proposal* was published over 50 years prior to this cartoon and features the cannibalism of Irish babies, not French citizens. Napoleon did not have an army in 1792 and the cartoon makes no reference to the military. The cartoon also does not depict any of the distinct classes that would make it a reference to the Haitian Revolution.

29. **(C)** Hugo is more supportive of the revolutionaries by framing their desires as noble despite their violence. Hugo does not ignore their violence, and Gilroy clearly opposes the revolution. Simply stating that one is a more "barbaric" depiction than the other is not the best choice as it lacks a historical focus.

Questions 30-32 refer to Topics 5.6 and 6.7

30. **(C)** The cartoon depicts diseases emerging from the River Thames in the form of starved children, being presented to the London city government (symbolized as a woman). This cartoon is meant to spur the government into addressing the social issues caused by industrialization. There is no mention of crime or prostitution in the cartoon, and it seems as if the city government (woman) is taking notice.

31. **(A)** In the 19th century, cities began investing in infrastructure to support the growing urban population, which included building sewer systems. Early suburbs were places for the middle class to escape crowded city life. Reforestation and carbon taxes are 20th century ways of addressing environmental damage, but not urban growth.

32. **(B)** Job shortages due to overpopulation led many Europeans to emigrate to the Americas in the 19th century. They did not emigrate to Eastern Europe. The number of children per family in Europe dropped without government regulations. There were not massive famines all over Europe—only in Ireland, and that was due to a potato blight, not overpopulation.

Questions 33-35 refer to Topics 5.4 and 5.5

33. **(D)** The British built the Indian railway system not for the population, but to allow Indian raw materials to be transported to ports where they were loaded on ships bound for England. While the population of India did grow in this period, it is not the reason for the growth of railways.

34. **(A)** Steam power transformed both production and transport during the Industrial Revolution. The British transported raw materials and not finished goods from their colonies. Railways were used to transport troops, but this practice was not evident until later, in the 20th century. The British and other colonial powers did not build infrastructure as a way to compete with rivals.

35. **(B)** Imperialism was conducted to ensure the economic domination of the imperial powers. Therefore, there was an effort to limit the industrialization of the colonized areas. The spread of Christianity was not an economic consequence of 19th-century imperialism, and democratic government was certainly not the aim.

Questions 36-38 refer to Topic 6.3

36. **(D)** The French author of Source 1 justifies imperialism through the lens of capitalism and the need for profit. he does not employ the concept of racial superiority or the need to compete with Britain. Communism was not widely seen as a threat in the 1880s.

37. **(C)** By the end of the 19th century, anti-imperialists were openly criticizing the actions of the colonizing powers. Imperialism and the disputes that arose form it became a major factor in causing World War I.

38. **(A)** By the late 1940s there was an increasing drive by colonized regions to fight for independence. Increasing questions about political authority and growing nationalism contributed to anticolonial movements. While some decolonization struggles were violent, they did not ultimately lead to world population decline.

Questions 39-41 refer to Topic 6.1

39. **(C)** The huge imbalance of battle casualties described by Churchill is due to Anglo-Egyptian army having vastly superior weapons, which Churchill alludes to when describing Britain as a "modern European power." There is no indication that the Dervish Sudanese were outnumbered, and no mention of the climate—though if the climate would have affected anyone, it would have been the non-native British. The French were not involved in Sudan at the time Britain sought to colonize it.

40. **(A)** During the 19th century, industrializing powers were establishing transoceanic empires, which makes this the best answer. While the Berlin Conference was diplomatic, it was an attempt to decrease conflict and was not the norm. While Africans had their own tribal/ethnic identities in the 19th century, it was in the 20th century that Africans would begin desiring nation states in resistance to imperialism. The U.S. was not a global power at this point, especially not in Africa.

41. **(B)** The main difference is that Kenya and Algeria attracted more white settlers than Sudan and Congo because their climate was similar enough to Europe that Europeans could raise plants and animals that were familiar to them. The colonizing countries did not know of the mineral wealth of a place until after they took control of it. All of the regions saw violence, and none were large markets for industrial goods.

Questions 42-44 refer to Topic 7.5

42. **(B)** The British wanted control of the strategic and oil-rich lands of the Middle East after the collapse of the Ottoman Empire. They were willing to work with the French to achieve this goal and were not really interested in the Arab position. By this time the Ottoman Empire had no political power or military.

43. **(C)** Transfer of former Ottoman territory to Great Britain and France under the system of mandates was dictated at the Treaty of Versailles. This was a slap in the face for the Arabs who had aided the British in their North Africa campaign. President Wilson demanded self-determination for former colonies but was unable to achieve this goal.

44. **(B)** German colonies were also transferred to Great Britain and France under the system of League of Nations mandates.

Question 45-47 refer to Topic 7.7

45. **(B)** World War I was the first total war, as governments used a variety of strategies, including political propaganda, to mobilize the populations (both in the home countries and the colonies or former colonies) for the purpose of waging war. A method commonly used was to exaggerate national superiority.

46. **(C)** The French artist created an image that is reminiscent of the French Revolution when the Grand Armée was forced to fight against enemies of the revolution. The large French flag and the courageous young women are designed to inspire national pride.

47. **(C)** Victory Gardens were another example of total warfare, where every facet of the economy and population is used to support the war effort.

Questions 48-51 refer to Topic 7.9

48. **(C)** Both Lenin and Mao are critical of peaceful means of revolution (which includes legislative) and champion violence as the only way of achieving socialism. They both advocate against the class hierarchy—Lenin seeks the surrender of power by the bourgeoisie (middle class), and Mao's piece on the peasant movement specifically mentions one class (the peasant class) overthrowing another (landowning class).

49. **(A)** Both revolutions were preceded by moderate nationalist revolutions—the Russian February (March) Revolution of 1917 and the Chinese Xinhai Revolution of 1911. Communism promotes gender equality, and these revolutions advocated a radical change in women's status. Although there were some vestiges of feudalism, ending feudalism was not their primary focus—their focus was more radical than that. While the Soviet Union did send some support to the Chinese Communist Revolution, during the Russian Communist Revolution, a coalition of Western forces actively fought against it in the Russian Civil War.

50. **(D)** Both governments enforced repressive policies that negatively affected their populations, including collectivization of agriculture (which often led to food shortages), work camps, and executions of dissidents. Both economies pushed hard to change their agrarian economy into an industrial economy by focusing on industrial machines and basic goods (not luxury goods). Both societies became insular as they saw the influence of the capitalist West as a threat to maintaining communist control.

51. **(A)** The Mexican Revolution, which was in opposition to U.S. neocolonialism, primarily wanted to take back economic control of Mexico from foreign corporate interests. It was not a monarchy, but the corrupt regime of President Porfirio Diaz that was overthrown. While it did involve land redistribution, it was not socialist or egalitarian in its goals like the Russian and Chinese communist revolutions. The Mexican Revolution was led by secular leaders, not religious, and was also incredibly violent.

Questions 52-55 refer to Topic 7.4

52. **(C)** The answer can be found by carefully examining the graph. Europe suffered more than the U.S. during World War I, and its economy was in tatters with mass unemployment.

53. **(B)** The economic boom of the 1920s in America resulted in risk taking and eventually resulted in the crash of the stock market in 1929.

54. **(A)** Economic nationalism became the norm during the 1930s as nations tried to put up a protective wall of tariffs and discourage imports to spur job growth at home. This had a negative effect on economic growth.

55. **(B)** The Soviet Union was not part of the global economy as its command economy was designed to strengthen the production of food and industrial goods, and the Soviets did not get involved in foreign trade.

MC Test 3: 1200 to 2001

Question 1-3 refer to Topic 1.6

1. **(B)** The passage states that the "divine body and blood of Christ was spilled upon the ground," and that the relics of martyrs were disrespected, showing that the church the crusaders plundered was indeed Christian. The passage places great emphasis on the riches contained within the church and the city, which indicates the city was fairly wealthy and prosperous. There is no mention of Mongols, Muslims, or how the city was invaded.

2. **(D)** The main goal of the Crusades was to take control of the Holy Land (Jerusalem). During the Fourth Crusade, which is the subject of the passage, the crusaders were settled for a while in Constantinople and pillaged it, due to agreements that were made in Venice when they negotiated payment for their transportation from Europe to the Holy Land. However, they did not do this at the request of the pope or any other church leaders. The Mongols were not a threat at this time.

3. **(A)** The plague spread across Asia and Europe during the 1300s, leading to a sharp decline in population. There was no known cure, and most attempts at treatment and prevention had little effect. Agricultural productivity did not reduce but rather increased population. Air and waterway pollution due to manufacturing was not a significant issue during this time. Population growth did not lead to increasingly violent warfare.

Questions 4-6 refer to Topic 2.1

4. **(B)** It is clear from the passage that silver was coveted by the Chinese. In fact, China was sometimes referred to as "the graveyard of silver." This was at a time when many precious luxury goods, including tea and ceramics, were transported from Asia to Europe along the Silk Roads. Central Asia was a hive of merchant activity.

5. **(C)** The Mongol conquest of much of Asia made trade safer during the *Pax Mongolica*. To make the long, expensive journey worth it, merchants transported luxury goods.

6. **(A)** As trade increased, trading cities prospered in Europe and Asia. This was before the era of European Atlantic voyages. The Black Death was devastating, but it did not kill half the population. Naval technology advanced but overland trade was still of vital importance.

Questions 7-10 refer to Topic 4.2

7. **(D)** The author makes clear his disgust for the captured people, describing some as "images of a lower hemisphere," yet still feels sympathy for them, as he says "what heart could be so hard as to not be pieces with piteous feeling to see that company?" He does not mention the slave traders themselves or Christianity.

8. **(B)** The Portuguese were granted sole access to the West African coast by the Catholic pope in the Treaty of Tordesillas, which meant that the Portuguese could profit greatly through a monopoly on supplying slaves to other European countries (and themselves) who depended on slave labor on plantations in their American colonies. At this time, slaves were not needed in South African mines, and they weren't used as deckhands on European ships. While there were some slaves among the elite households of Europe, that number paled in comparison to the amount that were taken to the Americas.

9. **(C)** Leo Africanus describes Timbuktu as a place of cultural diffusion, when he describes presence and exchange of various cultural products from all over the world, including cloth from Europe and "diverse manuscripts." There is no mention of pilgrimage, violence, or intolerance.

10. **(B)** Timbuktu was located inland along the trans-Saharan trade routes, and became prosperous and culturally diverse because of the trade that took place there. It was not along the coast, and therefore not involved in Portugal's slave trade. Timbuktu would have been just as affected by the Black Death as any other city in West Africa, though evidence that the plague reached sub-Saharan Africa is inconclusive.

Questions 11-13 refer to Topic 1.4

11. **(D)** The Aztec collected tribute from conquered regions, and the image provides one record of it. There is nothing shown on the military's power structure, domesticable animals, or literacy rates (writing in pictographs does not equal illiteracy).

12. **(C)** The collection of tribute was a way the Aztecs asserted their power over and intimidated subordinate peoples. The image shows nothing of nationalism, glorification of rulers, or diffusion of American culture into Europe.

13. **(B)** The Aztec Empire relied on the centuries-old trade routes that criss-crossed much of Mesoamerica and even connected North and South America. Jade, turquoise, feathers from tropical birds, and cacao were some luxury goods that traveled great distances along the pre-Columbian trade routes. While we know the Aztec were highly sophisticated in their knowledge of mathematics, so much of their cultural history has been destroyed that it is difficult to make a direct comparison with the Abbasid. Bolivar's Gran Colombia was based in South America, not Mesoamerica where the Aztec were located. The Aztec Empire was smaller, not larger, than the Roman Empire.

Questions 14-16 refer to Topic 3.1

14. **(B)** The image depicts the samurai with weapons bared, wearing intricate armor, engaged in battle. It does not show much about the structure of government, though due the civil conflict that is portrayed, it doesn't seem that power is centralized. The image has nothing to do with China, and is too narrow in focus to reveal anything about Japanese social hierarchies.

15. **(B)** Both European knights and Japanese samurai pledged their loyalty and fought at the directive of their feudal lord, though it was only the samurai who viewed ritual suicide to be honorable. Both knights and samurai were religious and followed an honor code tied to their beliefs. Both knights and samurai had highly advanced armor and weaponry.

16. **(A)** Japan's economy was based on rice. In fact, samurai received payment in the form of rice. Japan was very isolated, and while there was some trade with their neighbors, their economy did not depend on it. Japan's economy would not become highly industrialized until the late 19th century. Chinampas were an innovation of the Aztec to grow crops in swampland.

Questions 17-19 refer to Topic 3.2

17. **(B)** Both buildings blend Islamic, Persian, and Turkic elements with those of conquered regions. The mosque is not a celebration of a military victory, as it was built about 100 years after the Ottomans took Constantinople (Istanbul). The Red Fort is for military purposes and is not a religious symbol. It is not apparent what type of labor constructed these buildings by looking at the images.

18. **(A)** It is clear from the blend of different architectural traditions that these buildings were used to demonstrate dominion over diverse populations. The imposing nature of these buildings signal that they were used more for intimidation than accommodation. There is no indication that they were trying to create a common belief system. At this time, most people were farmers, so employment was not an issue.

19. **(C)** Süleyman and Shah Jahan used these works of monumental architecture to legitimize their rule. Louis XIV did the same thing as he built up the Palace of Versailles into one of the most opulent palaces in the world. The Nazis did not build the Reichstag, they set fire to it, and destroying a building is not the same as building a structure. Controlling trade does not necessarily legitimize power.

Questions 20-22 refer to Topic 3.4

20. **(D)** While children who were taken by the Ottoman for *devshirme* (and used as janissaries) often became important members of the Ottoman government (forming their own distinctive social class), that is not the focus of the passage. The author spends most of the passage lamenting how the taken children would adopt Islam and forget the Christianity they were born into. The passage mentions nothing of the survival rates of the kidnapped children.

21. **(C)** The main threat to Ottoman rule was from the elite Muslim families who had lived in the region long before Ottoman rule and were looking for ways to regain the power that they lost when the Ottomans took over. Therefore, the Ottomans were hesitant to hire anyone with local ties who may use their position in the government or military to stage a coup. Instead, the Ottomans kidnapped Christian boys from the outskirts of their territories, who obviously had no ties to people or positions of power, to fill important government and military roles. They trained them from a young age, converted them to Islam, and cut off all ties to their family to ensure absolute loyalty to the sultan.

22. **(B)** The Chinese dynasties based bureaucratic positions on merit through the civil service exam. The Jews in Spain and Huguenots (Protestants) in France were driven out by their respective governments, not given special treatment. Buddhists in the Mughal Empire did not receive special treatment either.

23. **(C)** The Janissaries became a formidable group within the Ottoman empire and began to use their power and influence for their own benefit, often directly opposing the sultan.

Questions 24-26 refer to Topics 3.1 and 3.2

24. **(D)** Louis XIV is encouraging trade by establishing a council devoted to commerce and investing in colonial trading. Though tariffs are a common feature of mercantile policies, they are not mentioned in the passage. The passage does not mention the threat of foreign competition or industrialization (which had not yet begun in Britain at this point).

25. **(B)** Louis' investment in navigation and trading companies sparked French colonial holdings to grow in the Americas, India, and Southeast Asia. Industrialization did not begin in France until after the French Revolution, over 100 years later. The persecution of the Huguenots and Jews in France was not a result of economic policy. The Hundred Years' War occurred 300 years prior to Louis' reign.

26. (A) One long-term result of Western European mercantile economic policy is increased tension among European powers as they competed for colonial holdings around the world. France and Spain did not try to isolate Britain except for a short time under Napoleon. Most patronage of the arts came from the government at this time, not from individual merchants (that was the Renaissance). Diffusion of European religion had already occurred as a result of the 16th century explorations.

Questions 27-29 refer to Topic 3.2

27. (C) The passage was written by a merchant who is using a time of peace to make a profit from trade in sake and soy sauce. The passage mentions nothing about daimyo or the role of the emperor in the economy. There is also no mention of *zaibatsus* (which are not formed until the 19th century).

28. (C) Japan had closed off trade with most European nations to avoid Western influence, but did allow trade with the Dutch. The Japanese were interested in "Western learning" and the Dutch wanted porcelain and silk.

29. (B) China and Korea are close to Japan and had been their traditional trading partners, and they gave the Dutch special permission to trade in a limited region of Japan as long as they did not proselytize.

Questions 30-32 refer to Topics 5.1 and 5.2

30. (B) The revolution in France created a conversation about rights in society. Witchcraft had been a focus 200 years prior, and is not addressed by de Gouges. Louis XVI never passed a law further restricting women's rights. Marat was openly critical of those in power, not women.

31. (D) By criticizing the practice of treating women as if they are in a "state of perpetual childhood," Wollstonecraft is arguing that women are not believed to be rational simply because they are not expected to be rational. She says nothing directly about women being seen as ornaments. She does not discuss education either, though she is obviously educated herself.

32. (D) They are advocating for women to be given the same respect as men. There is no evidence of them wanting to overthrow the monarchy. They are arguing against patriarchy, not for it. They do not mention the philosophic salons, and salons did not focus on women's issues but enlightened philosophy in general.

Questions 33-35 refer to Topic 5.2

33. (C) The painting shows Pedro I surrounded by a crowd of common people who are all shown to be clearly united in excitement about Pedro's announcement of independence, not simply respectful. There are a few military commanders in the background, but they are not the main focus. From the looks of the people's clothing in the painting it appears they still share much in common with European culture.

34. (C) The Brazilian Revolution was fundamentally less of a change than the revolutions against Spanish control of Latin America, as the Portuguese royal family had settled in Brazil to avoid the Napoleonic invasion of the Iberian Peninsula.

35. (D) Millions of slaves were taken to Brazil to work on the lucrative sugar plantations, so slavery lingered longer because of the profit motive.

Questions 36-38 refer to Topic 5.2

36. **(C)** The passage illustrates that Indians felt that the British were increasingly in control, and purposely enforcing policies to weaken their culture. There is no indication that Indians want to do away with the caste system, as the passage indicates they want to preserve it. The passage indicates a hostility toward Christianity, but no tension between other religious groups.

37. **(C)** After the Sepoy Mutiny, Queen Victoria abolished the British East India Company and took direct control of India due to reports of cruelty by the British East India Company in putting down the rebellion. Indian independence would not take place until nearly 100 years after the mutiny.

38. **(B)** The primary goal of imperialism was gaining raw materials and markets. Britain discouraged industrialization in India and all her colonies in order to avoid competition with British-made products. Britain did not need rice for its population.

Questions 39-40 refer to Topics 6.6 and 6.7

39. **(C)** The British had a problem as mechanization of labor and a growing population led to a rising unemployment rate, especially among rural and skilled workers. Using Australia as a settler colony addressed this problem. Britain was not primarily concerned with communist influence at this time or in closing the income gap. The influenza pandemic was not until 1918.

40. **(A)** Settlers wanted land that they could call their own, non-settler colonies were the primary providers of raw materials to the mother country. Usually climate and fertile land were the determining factors for a settler colony, not the population.

Questions 41-43 refer to Topic 5.2

41. **(A)** Rhodes is making a racist argument that Europeans are superior, which justifies English imperialism is his eyes. He mentions God, but not in the context of spreading Christianity. He does not directly discuss industrialization or imperial competition.

42. **(D)** The author is saying that violence will not "win" Africa. The author is not talking about equality, religion, or economic policy.

43. **(C)** The Boxer Rebellion in 1899 was a reaction against foreign interference in Chinese affairs. The American overthrow of the Hawaiian monarchy is an example of one nation conquering another. The Fashoda Incident was a stand-off between two imperial powers, not between an imperial power and their subjects; same with the Moroccan Crisis.

Questions 44-46 refer to Topic 7.4

44. **(C)** The Brazilian foreign minister argues that the borders of France and Italy and the independence of Poland and the Balkan states should be respected. He is informing the Pope of Brazil's stance on the subject, not asking the Pope to take action. This letter was written 200 years after the Enlightenment, so those ideals were already well known by this time. Germany is not mentioned in this excerpt.

45. **(D)** Brazil's respect for national communities expressed in the letter is most clearly aligned with President Wilson's argument for self-determination. The League of Nations permitted the Mandate system, which ran counter to self-determination. He was not aligned with Lenin's communism, as he just wanted national borders to be respected, not property to be redistributed. The foreign minister does not want to blame Germany, as he states he is against political or economic restrictions.

46. **(D)** The only example of multiple nations coming together to set policy that would maintain international peace is the Congress of Vienna that attempted to restore order after the Napoleonic Wars. The Treaty of Paris was not designed to solve multi-national problems. Seneca Falls was a meeting of women activists, not international diplomats. The Triple Entente and Triple Alliance were arrangements for times of war, not peace.

Questions 47-49 refer to Topic 7.8

47. **(C)** The excerpt describes people being branded like animals. It does not describe the conditions in the camp or the separation of prisoners. It also does not discuss security or escape attempts.

48. **(B)** Farms were taken by the state in both Cambodia and Russia. The Battle for Grain in Italy encouraged farming with subsidies. The Corn Laws encouraged farming by raising prices. The Enclosure Movement lessened the number of farmers on the land.

49. **(D)** Both the Holocaust and Cambodian genocide were carried out by extremist groups who had political power. Population density was not a problem in the two regions. Neither event was directed against immigrants. While it is true that governments began taking a more active role in citizens' lives after the Great Depression, it is not the reason for the genocides described.

Questions 50-53 refer to Topics 9.1, 9.2, and 9.3

50. **(C)** In the chart, population and grain production are both increasing at a similar, quite noticeable, rate. There is no data about the U.S. or rainfall in the chart.

51. **(D)** India took action and embraced the Green Revolution, encouraging the use of genetically-modified high-yield crops and synthetic fertilizers. The One-Child policy was in China. India encouraged sterilization in marginalized communities, not abortion.

52. **(B)** The Great Leap Forward was about rapid industrialization, and it failed. The Great Leap Forward was not about population control. The Green Revolution was based entirely on scientific advancements in agriculture.

53. **(B)** The Green Revolution was meant to provide food for growing populations, not prevent population growth. It was not developed to reduce social inequalities or to reduce the use of chemical fertilizers (it encouraged the use of chemical fertilizers.)

Questions 54-55 refer to Topics 9.1 and 9.5

54. **(D)** Greater access to medical care throughout the world has both lowered birth rates and death rates. Women entering the workforce might choose to have fewer children, but that does not account for the change in death rates. The charts show no decrease in population, as the birthrate in both charts is always higher than the death rates. While warfare and poor living conditions have an effect on death rates, it is clear from the chart they did not cause a decrease in population.

55. **(A)** The rapid population growth in less developed countries depicted in the chart has put a strain on natural resources in less developed countries, especially because these countries' economies are still primarily agriculture-based. Migrations are not occurring from former colonizing countries to former colonies—the opposite is happening, where less developed countries often experience a "brain drain." As the birth rate draws nearer to the death rate in more developed countries, their population does not on average grow younger, but older. Increased access to education in less developed countries is not a result of population increase, but it is one cause of the reduced birth rate.

SAQ Set 1: Period 1200-1450 Question 1

a) **SAMPLE ANSWER:** One piece of historical evidence that supports Nehru's argument that the Mongols were powerful because of brilliant strategy rather than their size is the fact that as pastoralists, their population was often smaller than the urban settlements they raided. Therefore, they often used tactics of terror and displays of brutal cruelty (such as piling up mounds of skulls of previously conquered enemies) to compel cities to surrender before fighting even began.

Wording of prompt is used to stay on topic. The prompt asks about Nehru's argument, so his argument MUST be addressed in the response.

Full explanation provides evidence as to why Nehru's argument is valid.

[Other responses could include: Mongols built up reputation of razing cities and town that showed resistance, including major capitals of powerful states; Chinggis alone was able to unify the Mongol tribes unlike ever before into a highly-disciplined army.]
Topic: 2.2

b) **SAMPLE ANSWER:** One historical example of an Asiatic group other than the Mongols that invaded Europe is the Ottoman Turks. The Turks conquered Constantinople in 1453 and from there looked to expand their territory into Eastern Europe. Under the rule of Süleyman the Magnificent they advanced as far as Vienna, until heavy rainfall and low supplies forced them to turn around.

Wording of prompt is used to stay on topic.

The Ottoman Turks' invasion of Eastern Europe is explained with specific details (evidence).

Topics: 1.7, 3.4

c) **SAMPLE ANSWER:** One factor that likely shaped Nehru's view of the Mongols is British imperialism in India at the time. As an activist for Indian independence, Nehru opposes Western dominance and racism in his native India, and uses history to disprove the myth of Western superiority by glorifying the power of the Asiatic Mongols.

Wording of prompt is used to stay on topic.

The passage is referenced to provide support for the response.

Topics: 6.1, 6.2

Mastering AP World History   **142**

SAQ Set 1: Period 1200-1450 Question 2

a) **SAMPLE ANSWER:** One social continuity in West Africa in the period circa 600-1450 is a matrilineal society. Many West African tribes were matrilineal, where family name and inheritance were passed down through the female line. This remained in practice despite the introduction of Islam (as seen in the passage), and only really became taboo under Western imperialism in the modern era.

> Wording of prompt is used to stay on topic.
>
> Wording is used to indicate CONTINUITY.
>
> The continuity of the practice is explained.

[Another response could explain the practice of polygamous marriages.]
Topics: 1.2, 1.5

b) **SAMPLE ANSWER:** One cultural change in West Africa in the period 1200-1450 was the increased acceptance and practice of Islam. It had been introduced by the merchants who traveled the Trans-Saharan trade routes, and was adopted by both the ruling and lower classes. As Islam was adopted by more and more people, it not only changed religious beliefs, but also introduced literacy to the oral societies of West Africa, which resulted in the building of great universities and libraries.

> Wording of prompt is used to stay on topic.
>
> Wording is used to indicate CHANGE.
>
> The cultural change brought about by introduction of Islam is explained.

Topic: 1.2

c) **SAMPLE ANSWER:** One economic change in West Africa in the period 1200-1450 is increased involvement in Trans-Saharan trade. Technology such as the camel saddle and caravanserai and the cultural connection to the Islamic world made it easier for Arab traders to make the long journey across the desert to West Africa where they traded large amounts of gold, salt, and slaves.

> Wording of prompt is used to stay on topic.
>
> Wording is used to indicate CHANGE.
>
> The economic change is explained using specific details (evidence).

[Another response could explain the increased involvement in the Arab slave trade.]
Topics: 1.2, 1.5

SAQ Set 1: Period 1200-1450 Question 3

a) **SAMPLE ANSWER:** One similarity between the military technology in the Americas and in East Asia during 1200-1450 is the use of bow and arrows. Both the Aztecs and the armies of the Song Dynasty used these weapons, which were made out of plant and animal fibers, to avoid hand-to-hand combat and kill opponents over 100 yards away.

[Other responses could explain how both used axes, knives, or spears.] **Topics: 1.1, 1.7**

| Wording of prompt is used to stay on topic. BOTH sides of the similarity are explained using specific examples (evidence). |

b) **SAMPLE ANSWER:** One difference between military technology in the Americas and in East Asia during 1200-1450 was the type of material used for blades on weapons. The Aztecs constructed wood clubs that had inserts of obsidian blades, which were filed down to be sharper than metal razors. The Chinese used long swords made from steel.

[Other responses could include how the Chinese made use of gunpowder and animal-related war technology, or differences in body armor.] **Topics: 1.1, 1.7**

| Wording of prompt is used to stay on topic. BOTH sides of the difference are explained using specific examples (evidence). |

c) **SAMPLE ANSWER:** One reason for the difference between military technology in the Americas and East Asia is the natural resources available in both regions. The Aztec had unique access to deposits of obsidian (volcanic rock), which was so effective as a blade they did not feel the need to look for an alternative. The Chinese, on the other hand, had access to deposits of iron and other minerals needed to make steel, and had been perfecting the steel blade since Classical times.

Topics: 1.1, 1.7

| Wording of prompt is used to stay on topic. BOTH sides are explained using specific details (evidence). |

SAQ Set 1: Period 1200-1450 Question 4

a) **SAMPLE ANSWER:** One similarity between the Silk Road and the Indian Ocean trade routes is that they both facilitated the spread of technology. Along the Silk Road, paper technology was transferred from China to the Middle East, and along the Indian Ocean trade routes, maritime technology, such as the compass, made its way from the South China Sea to the Mediterranean.

> Wording of prompt is used to stay on topic.
>
> BOTH sides of the similarity are explained using specific examples (evidence).

*[Other responses (**for A as well as B**) could explain how both facilitated the spread of languages; both facilitated the spread of religions; both were used to transport luxury goods; both facilitated the spread of the plague.]* **Topics: 2.1, 2.3**

c) **SAMPLE ANSWER:** One difference between the Silk Road and Indian Ocean trade routes is that the Silk Road was more dependent on unified political protection than the Indian Ocean trade routes. The Silk Road thrived the most under Mongol protection and became exceedingly dangerous after the Mongol Khanates collapsed. The Indian Ocean trade routes were very successful despite being maintained mostly by independent merchants. Most of the Indian Ocean merchant sailors were Muslim, which bound them by a shared code of ethics despite their geographic origin.

> Wording of prompt is used to stay on topic.
>
> BOTH sides of the difference are explained using specific details.

Topics: 2.1, 2.3

SAQ Set 2: Period 1450-1750 Question 1

a) **SAMPLE ANSWER:** One way the polycentric global economy described in the passage changed during the time period 1450-1750 is how it expanded to incorporate the Atlantic trade system, linking the Americas to Afro-Eurasia through trade. Beginning in this time period, European countries set up colonies in the Americas, and then exported raw goods such as sugar, tobacco, and furs back to the Old World where they were manufactured into finished goods. From there, the manufactured goods would be traded throughout Europe, Asia, Africa and back to the American colonies.

Wording of prompt is used to stay on topic.

The prompt refers to the passage so the passage MUST be addressed.

Wording is used to indicate CHANGE, and change is explained.

*[Another response (**for A as well as B**) could explain how European countries used military force to enter into Indian Ocean trade.]* **Topics: 4.1, 4.3, 4.5**

c) **SAMPLE ANSWER:** One reaction in East Asia to changes in the global economy during the time period 1450-1750 is when Japan restricted trade with Europeans. Intimidated by the increase of European merchant activity and the Spanish colonization of the Philippines, Japan prohibited all trade with Europeans except the Dutch, who were allowed to trade with Japan once a year off the cost of Nagasaki.

Wording of prompt is used to stay on topic.

The reaction is explained using specific details (evidence).

[Other response could have explained: China also placed restrictions on European traders; both China and Japan expelled/persecuted European missionaries.]
Topics: 4.5, 4.8

SAQ Set 2: Period 1450-1750 Question 2

a) **SAMPLE ANSWER:** One similarity in how Peter the Great and Akbar the Great legitimized their rule is the use of monumental architecture. Both the Peterhof Palace and the Panch Mahal were absolutely massive and required a huge amount of resources and labor to construct. Peter and Akbar used these displays of grandeur as a way of showing off how much power they had.

> Wording of prompt is used to stay on topic.
>
> The prompt refers to the images so the images MUST be addressed.
>
> BOTH sides of the similarity are explained.

[Another response could explain how they both built new capitals to consolidate power.]
Topic: 3.2

b) **SAMPLE ANSWER:** Another similarity in how Peter the Great and Akbar the Great legitimized their rule is how they both waged war almost constantly. Peter the Great waged war against Sweden, the Ottoman Empire, and Persia throughout his rule, while Akbar the Great more than doubled the size of the Mughal empire across northern India. Constant war not only helped expand their empire's borders, but also intimidated rivals and helped project the emperor's power.

> Wording of prompt is used to stay on topic.
>
> BOTH sides of the similarity are explained.
>
> Full explanation illustrates why evidence provided is relevant to the prompt.

[Other responses could include: they both enforced law codes; they both collected taxes.]
Topic: 3.2

c) **SAMPLE ANSWER:** One difference in how Peter the Great and Akbar the Great maintained political power is their tolerance for cultural diversity; Akbar was much more tolerant than Peter. Akbar was a Muslim ruler over a majority Hindu population, and realized that he would only have the people's support if he allowed them to keep their traditional culture. Peter, on the other hand, ruled over a population that was largely homogenous. Peter therefore tightened his control over Russian culture, going so far as to tax men who kept their beards, as a way control the elites and, in his eyes, make Russia more competitive with Western Europe.

> Wording of prompt is used to stay on topic.
>
> BOTH sides of the difference are explained using specific details (evidence).

[Another response could explain how Peter the Great relied more on non-elites to fill government positions than Akbar.] **Topics: 3.1, 3.4**

SAQ Set 2: Period 1450-1750 Question 3

a) **SAMPLE ANSWER:** One economic change in the Americas in the period 1450-1750 was the intensification of cash crop agriculture. During the period, European countries began to establish colonies in the Americas as part of a strategy to acquire cheap raw materials. Massive areas of land were cleared and plantations were set up, worked mostly by African slaves. Large quantities of sugar, cotton, tobacco, rice, and indigo were grown and shipped back to Europe to be manufactured into finished goods.

> Wording of prompt is used to stay on topic.
>
> Wording is used to indicate CHANGE.
>
> The economic change is explained using specific details (evidence).

[Other responses could include: incorporation into the Atlantic trading system (and Pacific); introduction of mercantilism.] **Topics: 4.1, 4.4**

b) **SAMPLE ANSWER:** One cultural change in the Americas in the period 1450-1750 was the introduction of Christianity. When European countries, such as Spain, England and France, colonized the Americas, Catholic and Protestant missionaries traveled to the Americas to convert the natives. Many natives either converted outright or adopted some aspect of Christianity into their belief systems.

> Wording of prompt is used to stay on topic.
>
> Wording is used to indicate CHANGE.
>
> The cultural change is explained using specific details (evidence).

[Other responses could include: introduction of new languages, architecture, culture from Europe and Africa; creation of syncretic religions, languages, recipes.]
Topic: 4.5

c) **SAMPLE ANSWER:** One political change in the Americas is the fall of the Aztec Empire. The empire under Montezuma II fell in the early 1500s due to Spanish conquistadors who overtook them by using guns, rallying disgruntled subjects, and spreading smallpox that wiped out the majority of the population. With the defeat of the Aztecs, the conquistadors claimed Mexico as a Spanish colony.

> Wording of prompt is used to stay on topic.
>
> Wording is used to indicate CHANGE.
>
> The political change is explained using specific details (evidence).

[Other responses could include: the fall of the Inca empire; European colonization (Republica de Indios); rise of Comanche empire; formation of Iroquois Confederacy.]
Topics: 4.2, 4.4, 4.5

SAQ Set 2: Period 1450-1750 Question 4

a) **SAMPLE ANSWER:** One economic change in Europe in the period 1450-1750 was the creation of joint-stock companies. New maritime technology allowed European traders to go on longer, though riskier, voyages than ever before. Joint-stock companies, such as the British East India Company, were formed to reduce the risk of financial failure through being funded by many private investors. Governments, who did not want to risk losing public money on a failed expedition, granted charters to joint-stock companies to set up trading posts and colonies in the Americas and Asia.

> Wording of prompt is used to stay on topic.
>
> Wording is used to indicate CHANGE.
>
> The economic change is explained using specific details (evidence).

[Other responses could include: the rise of mercantilism; incorporation into the Atlantic trade system; incorporation into the Indian Ocean trade system.]
Topics: 4.1, 4.2, 4.3, 4.4, 4.5

b) **SAMPLE ANSWER:** One cultural change in Europe in the period 1450-1750 was the formation of Protestant sects. In the early 1500s, a Catholic monk named Martin Luther published a challenge to the Church against the practice of indulgences and other abuses of power. The Church excommunicated him, but he had followers that left the Church with him and together formed the first Protestant sect, Lutheranism. Soon others followed and formed their own branches of Protestantism, such as the Calvinists, Anabaptists, and Methodists.

> Wording of prompt is used to stay on topic.
>
> Wording is used to indicate CHANGE.
>
> The cultural change is explained using specific details (evidence).

[Another response could explain the Scientific Revolution.] **Topics: 4.3, 4.5**

c) **SAMPLE ANSWER:** One political change in Europe in the period 1450-1750 is the rise of national monarchies. After the wars and plagues of the 1300s, the power of feudal lords and the Catholic Church was weakened. By the end of the 1400s, monarchs such as Henry VII of England and Ferdinand and Isabella of Spain took advantage of the political chaos by consolidating their power. These monarchs strengthened their control through direct taxation, maintaining standing armies, and marriages of political alliance.

> Wording of prompt is used to stay on topic.
>
> Wording is used to indicate CHANGE.
>
> The political change is explained using specific details (evidence).

[Another response could explain the creation of trading post and maritime empires.]
Topics: 4.2, 4.3, 4.4, 4.5, 4.6

SAQ Set 3: Period 1750-1900 Question 1

a) **SAMPLE ANSWER:** One piece of historical evidence that would support Wood's argument that the American Revolution was socially radical is the fact that after the revolution, the was no longer a traditional aristocracy. With a republic replacing the monarchy, old feudal titles no longer held any power or privilege. Political participation was possible for the common person, which was totally unique at the time.

> Wording of prompt is used to stay on topic.
>
> The prompt refers to the passage so the passage MUST be addressed.
>
> Wording is used to illustrate CHANGE, and change is explained.

[Another response could describe the radical nature of individual rights (rather than obligations) being guaranteed in the constitution] **Topic: 5.2**

b) **SAMPLE ANSWER:** One piece of historical evidence that would challenge Wood's argument that the American Revolution was socially radical is the fact that gender hierarchy remained unchanged. Women continued to be seen as inferior to men, despite their participation in the revolution. In fact, women did not receive the right to vote in the United States until the 1900s.

> Wording of prompt is used to stay on topic.
>
> The prompt refers to the passage so the passage MUST be addressed.
>
> Wording is used to indicate CONTINUITY, and the continuity is explained.

[Other responses could include: voting was initially restricted to white property owners; chattel slavery was still legal and slaves were not equal under the law] **Topic: 5.2**

c) **SAMPLE ANSWER:** One revolution that Wood is most likely referring to when depicting revolutions in other nations as violent and chaotic is the French Revolution. There was a period of the French Revolution specifically called the "Reign of Terror" due to the incredible violence against the population. The leader at the time, Robespierre, was paranoid about enemies of the revolution and tens of thousands of French citizens were executed in Paris and the French countryside.

> Wording of prompt is used to stay on topic.
>
> The prompt refers to the passage so the passage MUST be addressed.
>
> The violence of the revolution is explained in detail (evidence).

[Other responses could include: Haitian Revolution; Mexican Revolution (either one); most other revolutions (except Brazil)...] **Topic: 5.2**

SAQ Set 3: Period 1750-1900 Question 2

a) **SAMPLE ANSWER:** One way the passage reflects an economic continuity since 1550 is through its mention of plantation agriculture. Since the 1500s, European countries such as Britain colonized parts of the New World and set up plantations for growing cash crops such as sugar and tobacco. These raw materials would then be shipped to the mother country for processing and sale as finished goods.

> Wording of prompt is used to stay on topic.
>
> The prompt refers to the passage so the passage MUST be addressed.
>
> Wording is used to indicate CONTINUITY, and the continuity is explained.

[Other responses could include: use of slave labor in colonies; Atlantic trade.]
Topics: 4.5, 4.8

b) **SAMPLE ANSWER:** One reason why the slave labor mentioned in the passage was abolished by Britain in the 19th century was that it was becoming less profitable. As Britain industrialized, its economy became more reliant on goods mass-produced in factories. A larger market was needed to buy the goods produced. Paying free workers low wages ultimately cost less for business owners than slave labor while also expanding the market.

> Wording of prompt is used to stay on topic.
>
> The prompt refers to the passage so the passage MUST be addressed.
>
> The reaction is explained using specific details (evidence).

[Other responses could include: Christian/humanitarian opposition; slave uprising and escapes made slavery more costly.] **Topics: 5.1, 5.7, 5.9, 5.10**

c) **SAMPLE ANSWER:** Another economic change in Britain during the period 1750-1900 was the rise of capitalism. During this time period, Adam Smith's influential book *Wealth of Nations* argued against government interference in the economy. Many industrialized Western countries abandoned mercantilist policies in favor of unregulated, market-controlled economies. The adoption of capitalism led to a huge growth in wealth but also harsh labor conditions and periods of economic boom and bust.

> Wording of prompt is used to stay on topic.
>
> The prompt refers to the passage so the passage MUST be addressed.
>
> Wording is used to indicate CHANGE, and the change is explained.

[Another response could explain how women and children become part of the wage labor force.] **Topics: 5.3, 5.4, 5.7**

SAQ Set 3: Period 1750-1900 Question 3

a) **SAMPLE ANSWER:** One similarity between European imperialism in Australia and European imperialism in Central Africa was that both places were used as sources of raw materials. Australia was a source of precious stones and metals, coal, and iron. Central Africa was also a source of minerals, as well as rubber.

Wording of prompt is used to stay on topic.

BOTH sides of the similarity are explained using specific examples (evidence).

[Another response could explain how native populations in both places were treated harshly, killed, and coerced into labor.] **Topics: 6.1, 6.2, 6.4, 6.6**

b) **SAMPLE ANSWER:** One difference between European imperialism in Australia and European imperialism in Central Africa was that Australia was used as a settler colony, with a large number of Europeans living there, whereas relatively few Europeans actually lived in Central Africa. As a settler colony, Australia had a diversified economy and infrastructure that improved the quality of life. Central African colonies were set up simply to efficiently export raw materials and therefore there was very little invested into elevating the standard of living.

Wording of prompt is used to stay on topic.

BOTH sides of the difference are explained using specific details (evidence).

Topics: 6.1, 6.2, 6.4, 6.6

c) **SAMPLE ANSWER:** One reason why Australia had more white settlers than Central Africa was because Australia has a climate more similar to Europe. In Central Africa, European crops did not grow very well and Europeans were susceptible to diseases like malaria. It was easier and more comfortable for Europeans and their traditional crops and livestock to survive in Australia, which in certain regions has a more temperate climate.

Wording of prompt is used to stay on topic.

The prompt refers to the difference so the difference MUST be addressed.

BOTH sides of the difference are explained using specific details (evidence).

Topics: 6.1, 6.2, 6.4, 6.6

SAQ Set 3: Period 1750-1900 Question 4

a) **SAMPLE ANSWER:** One similarity between industrialization in Russia and industrialization in Japan during the period 1750-1900 was that the governments of both countries heavily sponsored industrialization. Both governments invested large amounts of state money in infrastructure, such as the Trans-Siberian Railroad, and factories. This happened because neither Russia nor Japan had a large middle class that was willing to invest in industrialization, like in Western Europe and the U.S.

> Wording of prompt is used to stay on topic.
>
> BOTH sides of the similarity are explained using specific details (evidence).

[Other responses could include: both industrialized in response to Western European expansion; both relied on foreign experts and technology; both ended serfdom to free up labor force; both were expansionist in seeking new land to aid industrialization]
Topics: 5.4, 5.6, 5.7, 5.8, 5.10

b) **SAMPLE ANSWER:** One difference between industrialization in Russia and industrialization in Japan during the period 1750-1900 was that Japan was more successful at industrialization than Russia. Russia was able to produce a lot of steel and textiles, but that was simply because of its size, not because of efficiency. Japan, on the other hand, was able to use technology effectively and quickly built a modern, powerful military that was even able to defeat Russia for control of Manchuria and Korea.

> Wording of prompt is used to stay on topic.
>
> BOTH sides of the similarity are explained using specific details (evidence).

[Other responses could include: Japan relied more on export of manufactured goods than Russia; Japan was able to phase-out state control of industries to private enterprises]
Topics: 5.4, 5.6, 5.7, 5.8, 5.10

c) **SAMPLE ANSWER:** One reason why Japan was more successful at industrialization than Russia is due to size. Russia's large size compared to its population made fast transportation of goods and people very costly and difficult. Japan, on the other hand, being much smaller, was able to more quickly construct railroads and infrastructure to connect its population and transport goods.

> Wording of prompt is used to stay on topic.
>
> The prompt refers to the difference so the difference MUST be addressed.
>
> BOTH sides of the difference are explained using specific details (evidence).

[Another response could explain how Japan's samurai class, no longer used in government, provided an educated, wealthy class of business leaders.] **Topics: 5.4, 5.6, 5.7, 5.8, 5.10**

SAQ Set 4: Period 1900-2001 Question 1

a) **SAMPLE ANSWER:** One economic change during the 20th century that is reflected in the passage is the emergence of multinational corporations. Multinational corporations, which produce and sell goods in multiple countries, were possible in the 20th century partly because of advances in transportation and technology that allowed goods to be produced and moved more efficiently than ever before. *Coca-Cola* is one of the most notable ones, as the passage notes that the company operates in "more than two hundred territories" throughout the world.

> Wording of prompt is used to stay on topic.
>
> Wording is used to indicate CHANGE, and change is explained.
>
> The prompt refers to the passage so the passage MUST be addressed.

[Another response could explain the emergence of free-market economic policies in the late 20th century.] **Topics: 9.1, 9.4, 9.8**

b) **SAMPLE ANSWER:** One cultural change during the 20th century that is reflected in the passage is the emergence of globalized popular and consumer culture. As noted in the passage, *Coca-Cola* is one of the most widely known products worldwide. This happened in the 20th century due to the U.S. using trade policy to influence foreign countries and gain support during the Cold War, which connected much of the world economically and spread U.S. culture.

> Wording of prompt is used to stay on topic.
>
> Wording is used to indicate CHANGE, and change is explained.
>
> The prompt refers to the passage so the passage MUST be addressed.

Topics: 9.1, 9.4, 9.6

c) **SAMPLE ANSWER:** One reaction to the globalization described in the passage are organized protests against the WTO and other inter-governmental organizations. Many people criticize globalization as destroying local cultures and exploiting the poorest countries. In 1999, there was a massive protest against the WTO conference in Seattle, where tens of thousands of protestors clashed with police.

> Wording of prompt is used to stay on topic.
>
> The prompt refers to the passage so the passage MUST be addressed.
>
> The reaction is explained using specific details (evidence).

[Other responses could include: economic nationalism; increased religious fundamentalism; anti-Western terrorism.] **Topics: 9.4, 9.7**

SAQ Set 4: Period 1900-2001 Question 2

a) **SAMPLE ANSWER:** One common historical process in the 20th century that is reflected in both passages is anti-imperialism. Ho Ci Minh states that one of his primary goals is to "overthrow French imperialism," and Kwame Nkrumah makes an argument that imperialism can only be stopped if Africa unifies itself.

> Wording of prompt is used to stay on topic.
>
> The prompt refers to the passage so the passage MUST be addressed.
>
> BOTH sides of the common historical process are explained using specific details (evidence).

Topic: 8.5

b) **SAMPLE ANSWER:** One difference in the goals of Ho Chi Minh and Kwame Nkrumah was that Nkrumah's movement was transnational while Ho Chi Minh was only concerned with the Vietnamese nation. Nkrumah wanted the leaders of the newly independent, sovereign African states to form their own intergovernmental body. Ho Chi Minh simply wanted to reunify North and South Vietnam, which had been separated after World War II.

> Wording of prompt is used to stay on topic.
>
> BOTH sides of the difference are explained using specific details (evidence).

Topics: 8.3, 8.4, 8.5

c) **SAMPLE ANSWER:** One reason why Kwame Nkrumah was ultimately unsuccessful in achieving his goal of uniting all of Africa is due to the development of nationalism in African states. African states inherited their borders from colonial territories, which paid no mind to traditional tribal borders. National identities were fostered first in the fight for independence, and then used by leaders to legitimize their rule and ease tribal tensions within their own countries. The idea of national identity ran counter to Pan-Africanism.

> Wording of prompt is used to stay on topic.
>
> Full explanation illustrates why evidence provided is relevant to the prompt.

[Other responses could include: sheer diversity of African peoples; lack of trust between African leaders; sabotage from the West due to Nkrumah's communist sympathies.]
Topic: 8.6

SAQ Set 4: Period 1900-2001 Question 3

a) **SAMPLE ANSWER:** One economic change in Latin America in the 20th century was the adoption of a corporatist economy in Brazil in the 1930s. The Great Depression hit Brazil especially hard, as its economy relied on exports of raw materials that dropped in global demand during the Depression. Through corporatism, the Brazilian government helped rebuild the economy by funding large industrial projects and using collective bargaining to settle labor disputes.

> Wording of prompt is used to stay on topic.
>
> Wording is used to indicate CHANGE.
>
> The economic change is explained using specific details (evidence).

[Other responses could include: Cuba's adoption of communism; Mexico joined NAFTA agreement with Canada and US.] **Topics: 7.1, 7.4, 8.4**

b) **SAMPLE ANSWER:** One political change in Latin America in the 20th century was Cuba's adoption of communism. Revolutionaries, upset by how much economic power the U.S. had in Cuba, overthrew the authoritarian President Batista. The revolutionary movement's leader, Fidel Castro, then came to rule Cuba and turned it into a communist country

> Wording of prompt is used to stay on topic.
>
> Wording is used to indicate CHANGE.
>
> The political change is explained using specific details (evidence).

[Another response could have explained Mexico's revolution against neocolonialism.]
Topic: 8.2

c) **SAMPLE ANSWER:** One cultural continuity in Latin America in the 20th century is that the population is still predominantly Catholic. Despite many Latin American governments' attempt at reducing the power and influence of the Church, the population is still majority Catholic, and is in fact home to more Catholics than any other region of the world.

> Wording of prompt is used to stay on topic.
>
> Wording is used to indicate CONTINUITY.
>
> The cultural continuity is explained using specific details (evidence).

[Other responses could include: population is still predominantly Catholic; Spanish/Portuguese-speaking; heavily influenced by Iberian culture, art, architecture, music, cuisine.]
Topics: 9.6, 9.7, 9.9

SAQ Set 4: Period 1900-2001 Question 4

a) **SAMPLE ANSWER:** One environmental change in South Asia in the 20th century is the introduction of genetically modified organisms (GMOs) and chemical fertilizers. The Green Revolution, as it is called, increased agricultural production tremendously, though the new crops negatively affected biodiversity and runoff from the fertilizer polluted waterways.

> Wording of prompt is used to stay on topic.
>
> Wording is used to indicate CHANGE.
>
> The environmental change is explained using specific details (evidence).

[Other responses could include: population growth puts strain on natural habitats; industrialization has increased pollution of air and water.] **Topics: 9.2, 9.3**

b) **SAMPLE ANSWER:** One political change in South Asia in the 20th century is the end of British imperialism in South Asia. In 1947, due to the build-up of violent mutinies, peaceful protests, and diplomatic negotiations, Britain finally granted India independence, ending centuries of British colonialism in South Asia.

> Wording of prompt is used to stay on topic.
>
> Wording is used to indicate CHANGE.
>
> The political change is explained using specific details (evidence).

[Other responses could include: the partition of India and Pakistan; women given access to political participation.] **Topics: 7.1, 8.5, 8.6**

c) **SAMPLE ANSWER:** One cultural continuity in South Asia in the 20th century is the continued influence of the caste system. Even though it was outlawed in 1950, the caste system is so ingrained culturally in India that in many rural areas, "untouchables" are still segregated from society and not allowed to interact with people of higher caste.

> Wording of prompt is used to stay on topic.
>
> Wording is used to indicate CONTINUITY.
>
> The cultural continuity is explained using specific details (evidence).

[Other responses could include: population is still predominantly Hindu and Muslim; European (British) influence from colonization remains.]

Topics: 8.6, 8.7, 9.6

Document-Based Question Answer Key

Use the rubric below to score your DBQ essays. But first, make sure to read through the annotated sample essay to see an example of what your DBQ could look like and learn how it's scored.

AP World History DBQ Rubric

CONTEXTUALIZATION Describes the broader historical context relevant to the prompt and relates the topic of the prompt to broader historical events, developments, or processes that occur before or during the time frame of the question.

THESIS Responds to the prompt with a historically defensible thesis/claim that establishes a line of reasoning.

EVIDENCE	1	2	3	4	5	6	7
Uses the content of at least three documents to address the topic of the prompt.							
Uses the content of at least six documents to <u>support an argument</u> in response to the prompt.							
Uses at least one piece of specific historical evidence (beyond that found in the documents) relevant to an argument that addresses the prompt. Evidence must be described and must be more than a phrase or reference.							

SOURCING & COMPLEXITY	1	2	3	4	5	6	7
For at least three documents, explains **how or why** the document's point of view, purpose, historical situation and/or audience is relevant to an argument that addresses the prompt.							
Demonstrates complex understanding of the topic by using evidence to corroborate, qualify, or modify an argument that addresses the question.							

/7

DBQ 1: Annotated and Scored Sample Essay

Prompt: Evaluate the extent to which increasing interactions among societies during the period 1200 to 1550 contributed to diffusion.

By the 13th century, interactions between states and empires in Afro Eurasia had increased due to a rise in long-distance trade along the Silk Roads and the trans Saharan trade routes. Luxury goods from East Asia, India and Africa were transported by merchants who met and exchanged not only goods and payment, but also cultural beliefs in growing trading cities such as Samarkand, Mombasa, and Kiev. After the Mongol conquests in Asia, the Silk Roads became even more active as the Mongols encouraged trade. Interactions led to much cultural diffusion as religions spread with merchants and missionaries. This was a long-term effect as these religions continued to thrive for centuries after their initial arrival. Languages were also spread as merchants and bureaucrats needed to deal with diverse populations.	Response earns the context point due to the idea of merchants exchanging cultural beliefs along trade routes.
	Response earns thesis point because it sets up an argument that religions and languages spread.
By the late 13th century, the Mongols had become the dominant power in Asia, because they had contact with many different cultures, they were very tolerant concerning religion. Although their original beliefs were essentially animistic, they accepted other beliefs such as Islam, Buddhism and Christianity. In Document 1 this is evident as an emissary of the pope reports that Güyük Khan was welcoming of Christians and there were rumors that he might even convert. This document was written at a time when the Roman Catholic Church was intent on spreading Christianity and missionaries were sent into many parts of Asia to convert people of other faiths. By 1280, a Franciscan friar in Document 3, describes how he and his fellow missionaries had built a church in Beijing and had baptized over a hundred young boys into the Christian faith. He wrote this in a message to his superiors back in Rome with the intent of encouraging the Franciscan order to send more missionaries along the Silk Roads to work in China. In support of this document, Marco Polo, in Document 5, reports from China that the Mongol leader, Kublai Khan was welcoming to Jews, Muslims and Christians. In fact, the Khan's wife, Chabi, was herself a Nestorian Christian.	Topic sentence sets up an argument that increase contact fosters toleration.
	This paragraph successfully uses documents 1, 3, and 5 to support the argument in the topic sentence.
	The historical situation is correctly identified in doc 1, and the purpose of document 3 is correctly identified.
	Writer attempts outside information with the last sentence but does not explain how it is relevant to the prompt.
Elsewhere in Afro Eurasia there was also active cultural diffusion as noted in Document 4 where a Chinese historian records that in Syria, envoys from many states come together including those of Persia and China; he also reports that envoys from the late Roman Empire were sent to China with precious goods from Africa. In addition, the Christian Bishop of Syria explains in Document 6, that many local people had converted to Christianity, which had made its way from the Holy Land to Syria, and which was adopted by the Syrian king after a near-death experience in a storm. Religious diffusion had also taken place in Russia after contact through trade with the Byzantine Empire which resulted in the acceptance of Orthodox Christianity by the Rus. The monk Filofei (doc 7), is proud to predict to his Tsar that he believes Moscow will become the "third Rome," this following the fall of both the Roman and Byzantine	No argument is stated in this paragraph.
	Documents 4, 6, and 7 are used correctly.

159 Mastering AP World History

Empires.

In addition, the Buddhist religion spread from its origins in South Asia as it was transmitted by both traders and pilgrims. By the late 13th century, the form of Buddhism known as Zen was very popular in Japan, having been conveyed through mainland China The beliefs are reflected in the Japanese print. (document 2). As was so often the case the religion was adapted to a new people and thus began the Zen school, which strongly emphasized meditation, and balance. The painting was done to encourage converts to Buddhism as well as to teach the new converts.

A second type of diffusion that took place because of interregional contact was the transmission of languages. This is shown in Document 1 where the friar reports how both Latin and French were used by clerks of European descent who were working for the Mongol khan. This was because the Mongols had no written language and tended to use the services of literate officials from their conquered lands. Another example of the transmission of language is shown in document 3, where the Franciscan friar claims that he has taught his young Chinese converts both Greek and Latin which delights the Chinese emperor.

> The topic sentence sets up an argument that Buddhism spread by traders and pilgrims.
>
> Document 2 is successfully used. And the purpose of Document 2 is also explained.
>
> The topic sentence sets up an argument that language also spread because of trade.
>
> Documents 1 and 3 are used successfully.

SCORE BREAKDOWN
THESIS – POINT EARNED
- Thesis consisted of arguments that were clearly defined and historically defensible

CONTEXTUALIZATION – POINT EARNED
- Successfully set the context by explaining the exchange networks that increased interaction

EVIDENCE – ONE POINT EARNED
- One point earned for using content of at least 3 docs (docs 1, 2, 3, and 5)
- NO point awarded for using at least 6 docs to support an argument that responds to the prompt (docs 4, 6, and 7, and described but not linked to an argument)
- NO point awarded for using outside evidence to support an argument (an attempt was made with the mention of Chabi, but it was not sufficiently explained)

SOURCING & COMPLEXITY – ONE POINTS EARNED
- One point earned for sourcing at least 3 documents successfully (docs 1, 3, and 2)
- NO point is earned for complexity. Although there is one factor of complexity present, the use of documents in multiple arguments, the response is not nuanced in pointing out that those documents have multiple elements.

TOTAL SCORE: 4 PTS
Topics: 1.2, 2.1, 2.2, 2.5, 2.7

DBQ 2: Annotated and Scored Sample Essay

Prompt: Evaluate the extent that technological developments affected interregional connections between 1400 and 1750.

During the period of 1400 to 1750, many advancements to transportation technology were made. During this time period many countries tried to expand their influence either for trade or conquest. Europeans, especially, were blocked from trade with Asia because of the Ottoman control of the west Asia. Therefore, the more advanced a country's ships were, like caravels and galleons, the more powerful the country would become. The technological developments of this time result in more advanced sailing technology as well as stronger interregional connections between countries.

During the period of 1400 to 1750, there were many advancements made in the development of ships and navigations tools. These advancements made it easier for countries to both travel to other regions and to understand the terrain of the region. Document 6 presents a picture of a Spanish carrack. This was an advanced ship at the time of its creation and was used to trade with and explore other regions such as Asia and west Africa. This revolutionary ship was about to earn the Spanish and the Portuguese wealth through large amounts of trade. Another advanced ship the was created in this time period would be the Treasure ships of the Chinese. Zheng He had ships that were over 300 feet long, so big that there were gardens grown on board, allowing the Chinese to explore and map all the way to East Asia. Document 5 is a map of the Americas which was used by sailors to better understand the terrain of the new world. The historical situation of this document is that it was made 1513, near when the Americas were first discovered, and because of that, the map isn't very accurate because only a few ships have sailed there and returned to provide the map-makers with detail. However, this map was still used by sailors because it allowed them to better understand the waterways of the Americas making navigation easier. Document 2 also talks about navigations techniques such as using the constellations to navigate. The author of the document uses the North Star to tells the location of an island that a crew claimed. Document 4 talks about the tactical use of understanding the waterways of Malacca. In the document Albuquerque has been told to go to the Strait of Malacca and intercept trade. The purpose of the document is to show the advantage that can be had from understanding the waterways and being able to control regions by blocking routes from other groups.

This new age of navigation and more advanced ships also allowed for the transportation of other things such as religion and culture through different regions. Document 1 is written by Zheng

Annotations:

- Essay earns contextualization point for explanation of Ottoman control of trade.
- Thesis point is not earned here because "stronger interregional connections" is unnecessarily vague.
- The argument—technological developments made interregional connections easier— is supported with docs 6, 5, 2, and 4.
- Outside evidence is earned for explanation of treasure ships.
- Essay earns sourcing for doc 5, explaining the historical situation.
- Failed sourcing attempt for doc 4, lacks insightful explanation.
- Essay makes argument and supports it with docs 1 and 7.

He, admiral of Ming China, and he writes about how he didn't just bring soldiers and merchants. He also brought translators and missionaries. The purpose of this document is to show how he is trying to spread the Chinese culture to the regions he visits, with translators and missionaries, which will in turn improve China's interregional connections. Document 7 talks about the trade relationship between Spain and the Philippines. It talks about how the two regions trade goods with one another and when one region fails to transport their goods to the other it causes problem. This document helps display the economic relationship forged from advancements in transportation technological. As governor of New Spain, he wants to impress upon his superiors in Spain the importance of sending the galleons from Mexico each year.

> Essay earns sourcing for doc 1, explaining purpose.

> Essay earns sourcing for doc 7, explaining purpose.

In conclusion, technological developments during the period 1400 to 1750 involved advancements in both ship building, the techniques used to navigate, and the tools used to navigate. It also allowed for interregional connections that improved trade and allowed for cultural diffusion, especially religious diffusion, to occur between distance regions.

> Essay earns thesis point by setting out two arguments: improved trade and religious diffusion.

SCORE BREAKDOWN
THESIS – POINT EARNED
- Thesis (at the end of the essay) consisted of arguments that were clearly defined and historically defensible

CONTEXTUALIZATION – POINT EARNED
- Successfully set the context of Ottoman-controlled trade routes

EVIDENCE – TWO POINTS EARNED
- Two points for using at least 6 documents to support an argument
- One point for using outside evidence to support an argument

SOURCING & COMPLEXITY – ONE POINT EARNED
- One point earned for sourcing 3 documents successfully – one on the historical situation surrounding the document and two on the purpose of the author
- NO point earned for complexity. Although the response is well-written, there is nothing that stands out as nuanced or exceptional.
    - **Complexity *could have been earned*** if the essay had taken into consideration: the limitations of the technology, other effects not specifically mentioned in the documents, or drawn comparisons between the impact of technology on interregional interactions during this time period with the impact of technology on interregional connections in another time period.

TOTAL SCORE: 6 PTS
Topics: 4.1, 4.5

DBQ 3: Annotated and Scored Sample Essay

Prompt: Evaluate the motives for industrializing powers to establish transoceanic empires in the 19th and early 20th centuries.

Essay	Annotations
In the early 19th centuries the Western European powers of France, Britain, and Germany, along with the Unites States and Japan were all busy industrializing. As their economies grew so did the need for raw materials to fuel industrialization. This is when those nations began to look past their borders for materials, and this would lead to imperialism. Competition over imperialism would eventually lead to two devastating world wars.	Context point is earned because the response explains that industrialization and the need for raw materials is what caused imperialism.
Motives that drove imperialism varied. There was primarily a desire to outdo the competition as industrializing nations vied for control of large parts of Africa and Asia. The motive of acquiring harbors and refueling stations was important in the age of steam power, as was the desire of acquiring raw materials to fuel industrial production. There was also in some cases, a desire by the richer nations to "civilize" their colonized subjects.	Thesis point is earned as the response lists multiple arguments: desire to outdo, harbors and refueling stations, and to civilize.
Competition between industrializing powers was a prime motive for 19th and 20th-century imperialism. In document 1, Paton writes a plea to the British government to take possession of islands in the New Hebrides at a time when Britain needed new harbors for its ships and new resources for its factories. Paton advocates that the British government move swiftly in order to stop the French establishing a greater presence in this region. Similarly, in document 2, Jules Ferry justifies the French colonization of Madagascar and much of Southeast Aria in the hope that his nation will continue to increase its influence on the world economy. Likewise, in document 3, the newspaper advertisement reflects the precarious position that existed at the time, as Germany as a nation had existed for merely 20 years. The author is angry because he believes a recent treaty concerning African colonies has put the Germans at a disadvantage when compared to the British. Ironically after World War I, the German colonies that did exist in Africa were handed over in the Treaty of Versailles to their arch-rival, Britain. Also, Japan entered World War I, in part, to take German possessions in Asia, which they were allowed to keep after the war.	Topic sentence sets out an argument—competition. Documents 1, 2, and 3 are used to support the argument. Sourcing is awarded for document 1 – purpose, document 2 – purpose, and document 3 – historical situation. Response earns outside information for discussion of Japan's motive for entering World War I.
The second very important motive for imperialism in this era was the desire to obtain resources and safe harbors for refueling steamboats with coal and for acquiring fresh supplies of food and water. In document 1, Paton indicates that the colonization of the New Hebrides would provide British ships with good harbors and a ready supply of water in Efate, which would be essential on the long voyage between Britain and its colony of Australia. Jules Ferry, in document 2, extols the need for French colonial expansion in places like Tunisia and Saigon, to provide safe harbors and supply centers. John Hobson agrees in	Topic sentence sets out argument—resources. Documents 1, 2, and 6 support that argument.

document 6, by explaining that colonial holdings provide markets and will bring increased trade for their colonial masters.

    A third, and less important reason for imperialism in the 19th century, was the notion that the industrial powers needed to "civilize" the rest of the world. In document 1, Paton writes of the need to "civilize" the natives in New Hebrides and bring them to the true faith, Christianity. Ferry, in document 2, advocates the policy of mission civilisatrice that justified French domination of its colonial holdings by claiming it was the duty of "superior races" to civilize "inferior" races. This belief resulted in French colonization of most of West Africa and its practice of encouraging its subjects to learn French and adopt the French culture. In contrast, in document 4, Blunt is shocked by the superior attitude of the imperial powers, most especially the British, and refers to it as "the gangrene of colonial rowdyism". His reasoning is based on the conviction that the colonial powers have no right to occupy the land of other races, and he would like to convince other British subjects to argue for an end to the practice. Likewise, the cartoonist in document 5, also seems to scoff at the notion that one race had the right to "civilize" another. At a time when the United States was planning to seize control of the Philippines from the Spanish, the cartoonist shows that there was more of a need at that time for a fairer civilization at home in America where beating and lynching of African Americans was common even after the abolition of slavery. Another critic of imperialism can be found in document 7 when Vladimir Lenin, the communist leader of the Bolshevik Revolution, dismisses the idea that providing infrastructure like railways will result in cultural advantages for the colonized masses. He claims that colonial oppression leads to inequalities and consequently results in the oppression of the masses.

Topic sentence sets out an argument—to "civilize."

Documents 1, 2, 4, 5, and 7 support this argument.

SCORE BREAKDOWN
THESIS – POINT EARNED
-Thesis consisted of arguments that were clearly defined and historically defensible
CONTEXTUALIZATION – POINT EARNED
    -Successfully set the context by explaining context of industrialization and imperialism
EVIDENCE – THREE POINTS EARNED
    -Two points are earned for using at least 6 documents to successfully support an argument
    -ONE point is earned for discussion of Japan's motives.
SOURCING & COMPLEXITY – TWO POINTS EARNED
    -One point is earned for sourcing at least 3 documents successfully (docs 1, 2, and 3).
    -One point earned for complexity through continuous use of comparison as well as for contradiction.
TOTAL SCORE: 7 PTS
Topics: 5.3, 5.4, 5.6

DBQ 4: Annotated and Scored Sample Essay

Prompt: To what extent did reactions to the political and social order lead to changes in the 20th century?

Essay	Annotation
Europe spread its influence around the world in the 18th and 19th centuries through colonization and control of the global economy. However, European dominance began to decline throughout the early 20th centuries due to taxing world wars. After that period, colonies increasingly questioned the burdens set upon them and formed new ideals, creating change. Reactions to the political and social order led to extensive changes in the 20th century. Independence movements and transnational movements among former colonies challenged western domination. However, much of their progress was held back because of internal violence that occurred, often due to rivalries that had been built up under colonialism.	Essay earns contextualization point for explanation that world wars led to end of colonialism. Thesis point is earned for arguments on independence and transnational movements, and sets up complexity by framing internal violence as limiting progress.
Colonies began demanding independence from their colonizers as a response to the oppression they faced, citing European ideals of freedom and equality. Ho Chi Minh illustrates this point in Document 2 when he writes that the French have oppressed the Viet people and that this is not right. This is further corroborated by Document 4, where the Algerian Liberation Front proclaims that its goal, an "Algerian state" had finally been reached. Mass political change was created throughout the world as colonies started revolutions. Another such reaction was in India in the mid-1800's. The British colonizers' political dominance and social reconstruction led to tension in India and the Sepoy Rebellion that sought to drive out the British. This is much like the ones in Vietnam and Algeria, except that it failed.	The argument—independence of colonies—is supported with docs 2 and 4 Outside evidence point is earned for explanation of Sepoy Rebellion, and it adds nuance (complexity).
Some newly independent countries even led a push to establish transnational unity among colonized people of the world. Jawaharlal Nehru, in Document 5 explains nations must be able to exchange ideas freely and not be tied to just their former mother country. Jawaharlal Nehru, as India's first prime minister wants to ensure that his young country does not fall back under foreign influence. This push for strength through connectedness was also mirrored by Nkrumah in Document 6, as he states that neo-colonialism and poverty can only be defeated through "African Unity."	The argument—transnational movements—is supported with docs 5 and 6. Sourcing is earned on doc 5 for explaining purpose.
However, these new countries' hopes of becoming strong states no longer controlled by the West were often not achieved due rivalries from colonial times that led to internal violence. Colonized people were subjected to intense racism and classification by their European overlords, which allowed them to divide and conquer. When they were no longer in power, the social divisions remained. For example, the rivalries between Hindus and Muslims that became intensified under British rule in South Asia turned violent after independence. Hindus and Muslims turned on each other and millions were killed. Document 3 is written by the British Prime Minister to President Jinnah of Pakistan, responding to Jinnah's	The argument—that progress was limited due to internal violence—fulfills the complexity set up in the thesis. Docs 3, 1, and 7 are used to support the argument.

165   Mastering AP World History

request for assistance in handling the violence that broke out after the partition of India and Pakistan. It is clear from this letter that despite Pakistan and India's desires to be independent countries, the violence makes them vulnerable to continued Western influence. Another example of this is in Africa. In Rwanda, Belgian officials classified the people there as Hutu or Tutsi dependent on physical traits such as nose length (doc 1). Tutsis were seen by the Belgians as racially superior to Hutus, and a rivalry grew between the two groups. That rivalry remained after independence. In the 1990s, the Hutu President of Rwanda's plane was shot down. The Hutus blamed the Tutsis, and a genocide occurred. Document 7 describes this, citing an interview from a young Tutsi, who hid under a bed as her parents were killed by Hutus. The UN sent troops to Rwanda to stop the genocide and keep the peace. These examples show how newly independent countries were not as free from colonialism as they wanted to be, as internal violence from colonial rivalries left them weak and vulnerable to foreign intervention.

> Sourcing is earned for docs 3, 1, and 7 as their historical context is explained.

SCORE BREAKDOWN
THESIS – POINT EARNED
- Thesis consisted of arguments that were clearly defined and historically defensible

CONTEXTUALIZATION – POINT EARNED
- Successfully set the context by explaining what led to decolonization

EVIDENCE – ALL THREE POINTS EARNED
- Two points for using at least 6 documents to support an argument
- One point for using outside evidence to support an argument

SOURCING & COMPLEXITY – BOTH POINTS EARNED
- One point earned for sourcing at least 3 documents successfully – 1 on the purpose of the author and 3 on historical context of docs
- One point earned for introducing a complex argument in the thesis and expanding on it in the essay; also the use of outside evidence and sourcing adds nuance to the writing and contributes to complexity

TOTAL SCORE: 7 PTS
Topics: 6.1, 7.8, 8.5, 8.6

DBQ 5: Annotated and Scored Sample Essay

Prompt: Evaluate the extent to which government policies sought to affect demography in the 20th century.

    The extent to which government policies sought to affect demography in the 20th century is two-fold. First, totalitarians wanted to increase the population in preparation for future domination attempts. While later in the century, many developing nations, though not all, sought to reduce population pressure to improve the society.

    The end of imperialism is the context to this question. Early in the 20th century, colonies, like India, were pushing for independence. Then World War I caused the Germans to lose their empire and sparked an even bigger push, especially in Africa, for independence. Totalitarians, especially Mussolini and Hitler, would come to power on the promises of returning their nations to greatness. Their plans rested on large armies expanding the borders of their empires.

    Totalitarian government policies earlier in the 20th century attempted to increase populations by encouraging child births and forbidding abortions. It can be noted in Document 1 that the council of USSR forbade abortions in 1936 due to its harmful effects. The purpose of this document was to completely reduce the number of dangerous abortions that were hurting women. The historical context of this document was that Joseph Stalin was the leader of the USSR, as a communist he is in favor of improving the situation for women, but with the threat of Hitler next door, he also has an eye toward increasing the size of his army. A similar view can be seen in Italy. Mussolini, in Document 2 states that a woman's fundamental mission is to bear children, and that other work will only distract them. As the prime minister of Italy, Benito Mussolini wants to see his population thriving because he has plans to recreate the Roman Empire and need young men for his planned conquests of places like Ethiopia, so he encourages women to choose reproduction over work. The final authoritarian, Hitler (Doc 3), equates having children as a victory in the battle to improve the nation. Hitler thought the Germans were the master race, so of course he would encourage more births. Additional evidence that supports this notion is the fact that the Nazis set up special camps where 'perfect' Aryan men and women were sent for the purpose of making babies, essentially baby-factories, where thousands of children were produced.

    After World War II government policies on demographics did a complete reversal. Many countries, especially developing ones, encouraged fewer children in order to improve the lives of those that were born and to improve the standing of the nation. This change can be clearly seen using document 7 which shows the dramatic increase in the number of nations that implemented policies to lower their fertility rate between 1976 and 2001.

Essay earns thesis point for setting up two arguments. It also shows a complex understanding of two different forces working in this time period.

Contextualization provided is very weak (it fails to contextualize developing nations mentioned in the thesis), but just good enough to earn the point.

The argument—totalitarian governments attempted to increase the population—is supported with docs 1, 2, and 3.

Sourcing is earned on doc 1 for explanation of purpose and historical situation.

Sourcing is earned on doc 2 for explanation of purpose and historical situation.

Sourcing is earned on doc 3 for speaker's point-of-view.

Outside evidence point is earned for Nazi reproduction camps.

The argument—developing nations tried curb population growth—is supported with docs 7, 6, and 5. There is also complexity in the acknowledgment of a change over time.

Reduced fertility was probably greatest in China. This can be seen in Document 6 where the Central Committee of the Communist Party of China mandated the One Child Policy as China's population was nearing one billion. The purpose of this document was to keep the population of China under control because they were in danger of overpopulation. If there are too many people, and not enough resources, people in China will not be able to live in optimal conditions. It is interesting to note that only a dictatorial government would be able to put a policy like this into place. Similarly, India (as noted in doc 5) granted women free medical coverage if they have two or less children, or if they have more than two, they can receive free coverage after being sterilized. India, under Indira Gandhi, was trying to modernize and saw large families as a roadblock to improving education and health care and that is why this policy was put into place. An interesting aside to this story is that India forcefully sterilized over one million poor Indians at this time and caused a crisis in the government when it was revealed.

Sourcing is earned for doc 6 for purpose and historical situation.

Sourcing is earned for doc 5 for purpose and historical situation.

A second use of outside evidence explains backlash to forced sterilizations.

However, not all developing countries took such a severe stance on population control. One exception was Cuba. In communist Cuba, population control was not so much the focus as easing the domestic burden of women, giving them equal standing in society. Document 4 is a Cuban maternity law that guarantees paid maternity leave for women, which would make having children easier, thus affecting demography. However, in Cuba, women also have the right to get an abortion, which is not a policy that is usually seen under governments who really want to increase their populations, like fascist Germany or Italy. This can be linked again to communist philosophy, but also to the fact that many women supported the Cuban revolution and granting them reproductive rights and benefits is one way Castro rewarded them for that support.

More complexity, as an exception (Cuba) is explained.

Third use of outside evidence cites the legality of abortion in Cuba.

SCORE BREAKDOWN
THESIS – POINT EARNED
- Thesis consisted of arguments that were clearly defined and historically defensible

CONTEXTUALIZATION – POINT EARNED
- Minimally set the context by explaining what led countries to implement policies effecting population growth

EVIDENCE – ALL THREE POINTS EARNED
- Two points for using at least 6 documents to support an argument
- One point for using outside evidence to support an argument

SOURCING & COMPLEXITY – ONE POINT EARNED
- One point earned for sourcing at least 3 documents successfully – 4 on the purpose and historical situation of the document, 1 on speaker's point-of-view
- NO point earned for complexity. The essay contains some complexity in its argument, but an essay must be strong throughout to earn the complexity point. The essay's contextualization was simply too weak.

TOTAL SCORE: 6 PTS   Topics: 9.1, 9.2

Long Essay Question Answer Key

Use the rubric below to score your LEQ essays. But first, make sure to read through the scoring guide to see examples of relevant topics and strategies.

AP World History LEQ Rubric

CONTEXTUALIZATION Describes the broader historical context relevant to the prompt and relates the topic of the prompt to broader historical events, developments, or processes that occur before or during the time frame of the question.

☐

THESIS Responds to the prompt with a historically defensible thesis/claim that establishes a line of reasoning.

☐

EVIDENCE
1 pt. Identifies specific historical examples of evidence relevant to the topic of the prompt.
OR
2 pts. Uses specific and relevant historical evidence to support an argument in response to the prompt.

☐
☐

REASONING & COMPLEXITY
1 pt. Uses historical reasoning (e.g. comparison, causation, continuity and change over time) to frame or structure an argument that addresses the prompt.
OR
2 pts. Demonstrates a complex understanding of the historical development that is the focus of the prompt, using evidence to corroborate, qualify, or modify an argument that addresses the prompt. This understanding must be part of the argument, not merely a phrase or reference.

☐
☐

/6

LEQ 1A Answer Key

Prompt: Develop an argument that evaluates the extent to which belief systems and their practices influenced social structures in one or more societies during the period 1200-1450.

Point	Notes
Context (0-1 point)	Examples of context might include the following, with appropriate elaboration: • Christianity and Islam spread to new areas in Africa and Asia, influencing societies. • Hinduism in India was the basis of that society for thousands of years. • Confucianism and Daoism were the base of Chinese stability.
Thesis (0-1 point)	Responses earn one point by responding to the question with a historically defensible thesis that establishes a line of reasoning about how belief systems and their practices influenced social structures. Thesis statements need to demonstrate some degree of specificity regarding causation, OR comparison, OR change over time. Examples that earn this point include: • Belief systems influenced social structure differently in South Asia than it did in East Asia. Under the Indian caste system social mobility was unknown, while under the Confucian system, people could rise according to merit. (comparison) • Salvation-based religions greatly influenced the gender social structure. Both Christian women and Buddhist women were given more social freedom compared to earlier society. (change over time AND comparison)
Evidence (0-2 points)	Responses earn one point by providing specific examples of evidence relevant to the topic of the prompt. Evidence used might include explanations of the following: • Hindu Caste System; sati practice; Confucian Civil Service Exam; Christian convents; female Buddhist monks Responses earn two points by using examples of specific historical evidence to support an argument in response to the prompt.
Reasoning (0-1 point)	Responses earn one point by framing or structuring an argument addressing comparison OR causation OR change over time in evaluating how ideology influenced social structure. The reasoning used in the response might be uneven or imbalanced. Examples of using historical reasoning using comparison might include: • comparing how elites used different ideologies to maintain their authority • comparing how religion was used to maintain the status quo in two different regions • explaining how the arrival of new religions affected women's roles
Complexity (0-1 point)	Responses earn the complexity point by demonstrating a complex understanding of how ideology influences the social structure. Ways of demonstrating a complex understanding of this prompt might include: • Explaining similarities AND differences in how beliefs influenced the social structure • Comparing how beliefs influenced the social structure in the period stated with how they influenced social structure in another period • Using change over time to explain how beliefs influenced social structure in a continuous way, such as the Confucian ideology continuing throughout future Chinese dynasties, or the continued use of the Indian caste system in stabilizing the Indian social structure

Topics: 1.2, 1.3, 1.6, 2.5

LEQ 1B Answer Key
Prompt: Develop an argument that evaluates the environmental effects of the Columbian Exchange in one or more regions during the period 1450-1750.

Point	Notes
Context (0-1 point)	Examples of context, depending on the era of the question that the writer chooses to focus on, might include the following, with appropriate elaboration: • The bubonic plague weakened the Catholic Church • The intensification of conflict between the Ottoman and Safavid Empires increased Sunni-Shiite tension • The Ming dynasty reasserted Neo-Confucianism
Thesis (0-1 point)	Responses earn one point by responding to the question with a historically defensible thesis that establishes a line of reasoning about how belief systems influence political, cultural or social structure. Thesis statements need to demonstrate some degree of specificity regarding causation, OR comparison, OR change over time. Examples that earn this point include: • Both the Protestant Reformation and the Catholic Counter Reformation contributed to the growth of Christianity, especially in colonial holdings. (comparison) • Tension in India between Muslims and Hindus led to the creation of a new belief system, Sikhism, that tried to bring harmony to the region. (causation) • The Age of Enlightenment caused the new educated elite to challenge the political status quo. (causation AND change over time)
Evidence (0-2 points)	Responses earn one point by providing specific examples of evidence relevant to the topic of the prompt. Evidence used might include explanations of the following: • Martin Luther, 95 Thesis, Jesuits, Sunni, Shi'a, Sikhism, early Enlightenment, John Locke Responses earn two points by using examples of specific historical evidence to support an argument in response to the prompt.
Reasoning (0-1 point)	Responses earn one point by framing or structuring an argument addressing comparison OR causation OR change over time in evaluating how changing belief systems influenced political, cultural, or social structure between 1450 and 1750. The reasoning used in the response might be uneven or imbalanced. Examples of using historical reasoning might include: • comparing how belief systems enforced patriarchy • explaining the effects of religious rivalries on the government of a region • explaining how the loss of power by the Catholic Church impacted education
Complexity (0-1 point)	Responses earn the complexity point by demonstrating a complex understanding of how beliefs influence political, cultural, or social structure. Ways of demonstrating a complex understanding of this prompt might include: • Explaining similarities **AND** differences in how beliefs influence society • Comparing how beliefs influenced the society in the period stated with how they influenced society in another period, such as the age of revolutions in the next period • Using change over time to explain how belief systems influence social structure in a continuous way, such as the Confucian ideology continuing from the Song dynasty previously or how it continued to shape society in the Qing Dynasty of the next period

Topics: 3.3, 5.1, 4.7

LEQ 1C Answer Key

Prompt: Develop an argument that evaluates the extent to which industrialization influenced social structures in one or more regions during the period 1750-1900.

Point	Notes
Context (0-1 point)	Examples of context might include the following, with appropriate elaboration: • Explanation of social class in pre-industrial society • Explanation of the beginnings of industrialization
Thesis (0-1 point)	Responses earn one point by responding to the question with a historically defensible thesis that establishes a line of reasoning about how industrialization influenced social structures between 1750-1900 in one or more societies. Thesis statements need to demonstrate some degree of specificity regarding causation, OR comparison, OR change over time. Examples that earn this point include: • Industrialization created a new working class and caused the end of slavery; as well as causing the rise of the middle class. (causation) • Women's roles in society increased as they became essential as wage earners but remained the same in that they still were responsible for the management of the home. (change over time)
Evidence (0-2 points)	Responses earn one point by providing specific examples of evidence relevant to the topic of the prompt. Evidence used might include explanations of the following: • Factory work, wage labor, textile mills, why wage labor is more efficient than slave labor, middle class women, educational opportunities, servants, Consumerism, urbanization, growth of Manchester Responses earn two points by using examples of specific historical evidence to support an argument in response to the prompt.
Reasoning (0-1 point)	Responses earn one point by framing or structuring an argument addressing comparison OR causation OR change over time concerning how industrialization influenced social structure between 1750-1900. The reasoning used in the response might be uneven or imbalanced. Examples of using historical reasoning might include: • Explaining how quickly the working class formed and how important the growing middle class became • Comparing the quick end of slavery by the industrializing British compared to the slow end to slavery in a non-industrialized area.
Complexity (0-1 point)	Responses earn the complexity point by demonstrating a complex understanding of industrial influences social structures between 1750-1900. Ways of demonstrating a complex understanding of this prompt might include: • Explaining similarities **AND** differences in how industrialization influenced social structures in two regions • Using change over time to explain how industrialization did NOT influence social structures, such as the traditional role of women as caretakers did not change, it simply was added onto – the theory of the "second shift"

Topics: 5.9, 5.10

LEQ 2A Answer Key

Prompt: Develop an argument that evaluates the extent to which expanding empires affected trade in one or more regions during the period 1200-1450.

Point	Notes
Context (0-1 point)	Examples of context might include the following, with appropriate elaboration: - The desire for luxury goods led to the expansion of sea routes as well as land routes - With stable empires came long periods of peace and prosperity, leading to economic growth
Thesis (0-1 point)	Responses earn one point by responding to the question with a historically defensible thesis that establishes a line of reasoning about how expanding empires affected trade in the period 1200 to 1450. Thesis statements need to demonstrate some degree of specificity regarding causation, OR comparison, OR change over time. Examples that earn this point include: - The rise of the Mongol Empire fostered an economic revival of the Silk Road. (causation AND change over time) - From 1200 to 1450 empires, like the Byzantine and Mali Empires, encouraged trade in order to profit from taxation. (comparison) - The Ming Empire affected trade by encouraging the production of luxury goods, like silk and porcelain, in order to increase the amount of silver flowing into China. (causation)
Evidence (0-2 points)	Responses earn one point by providing specific examples of evidence relevant to the topic of the prompt. Evidence used might include explanations of the following: - *Pax Mongolica*, passports, luxury goods, Bezant, gold and salt trade Responses earn two points by using examples of specific historical evidence to support an argument in response to the prompt.
Reasoning (0-1 point)	Responses earn one point by framing or structuring an argument addressing comparison, OR causation, OR change over time in explaining how empires affected trade in the period 1200 to 1450. The reasoning used in the response might be uneven or imbalanced. Examples of using historical reasoning might include: - Change from a declining Silk Road to a revitalized one - Continuity in the desire for luxury goods - Similarities in the promotion of trade for taxation purposes - The effect of political stability on trade
Complexity (0-1 point)	Responses earn the complexity point by demonstrating a complex understanding of how empires affected trade. Ways of demonstrating a complex understanding of this prompt might include: - Explaining changes AND continuities in how affected trade - Using comparison to show how governments in another time period affected trade, for example, modern trade agreements like the EU or NAFTA - Consistently using cause and effect relationships when explaining empires influence trade

Topics: 2.1, 2.2, 2.3, 2.4

LEQ 2B Answer Key

Prompt: Develop an argument that evaluates the extent to which changes to the networks of exchange affected societies in one or more regions during the period 1450-1750.

Point	Notes
Context (0-1 point)	Examples of context might include the following, with appropriate elaboration: • Introduction of new maritime technology • European need to avoid dealing with the Ottoman Empire • Increased demand for luxury goods like sugar and cotton • Growth of Atlantic Triangle Trade
Thesis (0-1 point)	Responses earn one point by responding to the question with a historically defensible thesis that establishes a line of reasoning about how networks of exchange affected societies between 1450 and 1750. Thesis statements need to demonstrate some degree of specificity regarding causation, OR comparison, OR change over time. Examples that earn this point include: • Networks of exchange affected societies between 1450 and 1750. With the creation of the Triangle Trade system, African slave trade decimated West Africa by destabilizing local governments and upsetting the gender balance. (causation) • Between 1450 and 1750 networks of exchange negatively affected native societies in the Americas by introducing diseases, but positively affected Europe by introducing new food crops that improved nutrition. (comparison)
Evidence (0-2 points)	Responses earn one point by providing specific examples of evidence relevant to the topic of the prompt. Evidence used might include explanations of the following: • Triangle Trade, African slave trade, smallpox, sugar plantations, Haiti, Brazil, cotton plantations, corn, potato, peanut Responses earn two points by using examples of specific historical evidence to support an argument in response to the prompt.
Reasoning (0-1 point)	Responses earn one point by framing or structuring an argument addressing comparison, OR causation, OR change over time in explaining how trade networks affected society in the period 1450-1750. The reasoning used in the response might be uneven or imbalanced. Examples of using historical reasoning might include: • Explaining how some colonial societies became reliant on slave labor • Comparing the effect of trade on two places, like the American colonies and Europe • Explaining how African societies changed over time because of European slavery
Complexity (0-1 point)	Responses earn the complexity point by demonstrating a complex understanding of how trade networks affected society in the period 1450-1750. Ways of demonstrating a complex understanding of this prompt might include: • Explaining changes **AND** continuities, or similarities **AND** differences, or causes **AND** effects in how trade networks affected society in the period 1450-1750. • Using comparison to show how trade networks affected society in another time period, for example how the Muslim slave trade affected Africa prior to 1450.

Topics: 3.2, 3.4, 4.1, 4.2, 4.3, 4.4, 4.5

LEQ 2C Answer Key

Prompt: Develop an argument that evaluates the extent to which changes to the networks of exchange affected societies in one or more regions after 1900.

Point	Notes
Context (0-1 point)	Examples of context might include the following, with appropriate elaboration: • Increasing globalization • World War I's economic impact • Communist revolutions in Russia or China • World War II's economic impact
Thesis (0-1 point)	Responses earn one point by responding to the question with a historically defensible thesis that establishes a line of reasoning about how economic processes changed after 1900. Thesis statements need to demonstrate some degree of specificity regarding causation, OR comparison, OR change over time. Examples that earn this point include: • Economic processes changed after 1900. The Great Depression caused governments to put measures in place to regulate trade in order to favor their own economies. (causation) • After World War II, free trade agreements like the EU and NAFTA helped to create a new, globalized economy. (causation AND change over time)
Evidence (0-2 points)	Responses earn one point by providing specific examples of evidence relevant to the topic of the prompt. Evidence used might include explanations of the following: • Great Depression, economic nationalism, tariff, command economy, EU, NAFTA, free trade, globalization, *perestroika* Responses earn two points by using examples of specific historical evidence to support an argument in response to the prompt.
Reasoning (0-1 point)	Responses earn one point by framing or structuring an argument addressing comparison, OR causation, OR change over time in explaining how economic processes changed after 1900. The reasoning used in the response might be uneven or imbalanced. Examples of using historical reasoning using CCOT might include: • Explaining how economic processes changed society for the worse: depression, economic nationalism • Explaining how economic processes changed society for the better: tele-commuting, decreased poverty in some regions • Explaining the economic processes changed over time, command economies with less social freedom in most communist nations became free market economies
Complexity (0-1 point)	Responses earn the complexity point by demonstrating a complex understanding of how economic processes changed after 1900. Ways of demonstrating a complex understanding of this prompt might include: • Explaining changes AND continuities, or similarities AND differences, or causes AND effects in how economic processes changed after 1900. • Using comparison to show how economic processes changed areas in another time period, for example during the Industrial Revolution

Topics: 7.4, 8.4, 8.6, 9.4, 9.9

LEQ 3A Answer Key

Prompt: Develop an argument that evaluates how states gained and maintained power in one or more regions during the period 1200-1450.

Point	Notes
Context (0-1 point)	Examples of context might include the following, with appropriate elaboration: • A description of the weakening of states, prior to 1200, in the region(s) that is the focus of the student's essay
Thesis (0-1 point)	Responses earn one point by responding to the question with a historically defensible thesis that establishes a line of reasoning about how states gained and maintained power in one or more regions. Thesis statements need to demonstrate some degree of specificity regarding causation, OR comparison, OR change over time. Examples that earn this point include: • States gain power in very similar ways. Often states gain power because of a charismatic leader who unifies the state behind them. However, states maintain power in very different ways; some maintain power through centralization, while others maintain power by leaving regional leaders in charge. (comparison) • The Mongols gained power by using intimidation tactics that caused people to fear them. They maintained power using their military that could react quickly to threats. (causation) • The Ming Dynasty gained and maintained power through the use of Confucian ideology that rebuilt the bureaucracy and justified Ming rule. (causation AND change over time)
Evidence (0-2 points)	Responses earn one point by providing specific examples of evidence relevant to the topic of the prompt. Evidence used might include explanations of the following: • Genghis Khan, tower of skulls, cavalry, civil service exam, Confucianism Responses earn two points by using examples of specific historical evidence to support an argument in response to the prompt.
Reasoning (0-1 point)	Responses earn one point by framing or structuring an argument addressing comparison, OR causation, OR change over time in explaining how states gained and maintained power. The reasoning used in the response might be uneven or imbalanced. Examples of using historical reasoning might include: • Comparing two leaders who unified different empires • Describing the cause and effect relationship of unifying tactics • Explaining how one tactic was used continually during an empire to maintain power
Complexity (0-1 point)	Responses earn the complexity point by demonstrating a complex understanding of how states gained and maintained power. Ways of demonstrating a complex understanding of this prompt might include: • Explaining the changes AND continuities, or similarities AND differences, or causes AND effects when describing how states gained AND maintained power • Comparing how states gained and maintained power in another time period, for example how the maritime empires gained and maintained power in the next time period.

Topics: 1.1, 1.2, 1.3, 1.4, 1.5, 1.7

LEQ 3B Answer Key

Prompt: Develop an argument that evaluates how empires gained and maintained power in one or more regions during the period 1450-1750.

Point	Notes
Context (0-1 point)	Examples of context might include the following, with appropriate elaboration: • An explanation of the weakening of the states and empires that preceded those that would rise between 1450 and 1750. • An explanation of the economic state of the world in 1450 that would lead to the political changes of 1450 to 1750.
Thesis (0-1 point)	Responses earn one point by responding to the question with a historically defensible thesis that establishes a line of reasoning about how empires gained and maintained power. Thesis statements need to demonstrate some degree of specificity regarding causation, OR comparison, OR change over time. Examples that earn this point include: • The Ottoman and Ming Empires both gained power by using new gunpowder technology. The both maintained power with a state educated bureaucracy. (comparison) • Peter the Great, in Russia, grew in power during this period because the government took more control of the Orthodox church. He maintained his power by weakening the nobility. (causation) • The Mughals gained power by taking advantage of the fact that the Indians distrusted eachother. They maintained their power by using the existing caste system to control the Indian population. (causation AND change over time)
Evidence (0-2 points)	Responses earn one point by providing specific examples of evidence relevant to the topic of the prompt. Evidence used might include explanations of the following: • Osman Bey, gunpowder, cannon, *devshirme*, theme system, Civil Service system, patriarch, boyars, Babur, caste system Responses earn two points by using examples of specific historical evidence to support an argument in response to the prompt.
Reasoning (0-1 point)	Responses earn one point by framing or structuring an argument addressing comparison, OR causation, OR change over time in explaining how empires gained and maintained power The reasoning used in the response might be uneven or imbalanced. Examples of using historical reasoning might include: • Comparing how two empires gained and maintained power, such as the Ottoman and the Ming • Showing a cause and effect relationship, such as Peter the Great's domination of both the Church and the nobility in Russia • Showing change or continuity over time, such as the Mughal's use of India's historical and cultural heritage in order to control the conquered population
Complexity (0-1 point)	Responses earn the complexity point by demonstrating a complex understanding of how interregional interactions affected ideologies and belief systems. Ways of demonstrating a complex understanding of this prompt might include: • Explaining the changes AND continuities, or similarities AND differences, or causes AND effects when describing how empires gained AND maintained power • Comparing how empires gained power in the specified period, 1450-1750, with how empires gained power in another period, like the Mongols in the previous era, or the British in the subsequent era

Topics: 3.1, 3.2, 3.4

LEQ 3C Answer Key

Prompt: Develop an argument that evaluates how state power shifted in one or more regions during the period 1750-1900.

Point	Notes
Context (0-1 point)	Examples of context might include the following, with appropriate elaboration: • Enlightenment thought caused intellectuals to challenge current political norms • The Industrial Revolution caused a new round of imperialism • The Industrial Revolution caused workers to question the existing power structure
Thesis (0-1 point)	Responses earn one point by responding to the question with a historically defensible thesis that establishes a line of reasoning about how state power shifted during the time period. Thesis statements need to demonstrate some degree of specificity regarding causation, OR comparison, OR change over time. Examples that earn this point include: • In the period beginning in 1750, state power shifted as colonies in the Americas gained their independence. Some became democracies and others became authoritarian. (comparison) • State power shifted in the period 1750 to 1900 as European nation came to dominate Africa and Asia politically through imperialism. (change over time) • Near the end of this period, state power shifted toward the middle and working class as those groups demanded and won political power in much of Western Europe. (causation)
Evidence (0-2 points)	Responses earn one point by providing specific examples of evidence relevant to the topic of the prompt. Evidence used might include explanations of the following: • American Revolution, constitution, Brazilian Revolution, Haitian Revolution, Opium Wars, Treaty of Nanjing, Marx, communism Responses earn two points by using examples of specific historical evidence to support an argument in response to the prompt.
Reasoning (0-1 point)	Responses earn one point by framing or structuring an argument addressing comparison, OR causation, OR change over time in explaining how state power shifted during the time period. The reasoning used in the response might be uneven or imbalanced. Examples of using historical reasoning might include: • While the new United States became a democracy, Brazil became a kingdom. • Britain, France, and the Netherlands began to slowly colonize the coastal regions of Africa, and South Asia eventually taking full control. • As the working and middle class became more educated, they began to agitate for more power.
Complexity (0-1 point)	Responses earn the complexity point by demonstrating a complex understanding of how state power shifted during the time period. Ways of demonstrating a complex understanding of this prompt might include: • Explaining the changes **AND** continuities, or similarities **AND** differences, or causes **AND** effects when describing how state power shifted during the time period. • Comparing how state power shifted in a previous period, such as the rise of the west during the age of discovery in the previous period. •

Topics: 5.1, 5.2, 5.8, 6.1, 6.2

LEQ 4A Answer Key

Prompt: Develop an argument that evaluates the environmental effects of the networks of exchange in one or more regions during the period 1200-1450.

Point	Notes
Context (0-1 point)	Examples of context might include the following, with appropriate elaboration: • Explain how the growing wealth of societies causes increasing long distance contact • Explain how increasingly peaceful travel aides in the diffusion of goods, ideas, as well as disease
Thesis (0-1 point)	Responses earn one point by responding to the question with a historically defensible thesis that establishes a line of reasoning about the environmental effects of networks of exchange. Thesis statements need to demonstrate some degree of specificity regarding causation, OR comparison, OR change over time. Examples that earn this point include: • In the period 1200 to 1450 there was a continuous diffusion of crops and disease along the trade networks. (change over time) • Between 1200 and 1450 European and Arab merchants along the trade routes needed to understand wind patterns as well as ocean currents. (comparison)
Evidence (0-2 points)	Responses earn one point by providing specific examples of evidence relevant to the topic of the prompt. Evidence used might include explanations of the following: • Cotton, citrus, bubonic plague, *volta do mar*, monsoons Responses earn two points by using examples of specific historical evidence to support an argument in response to the prompt.
Reasoning (0-1 point)	Responses earn one point by framing or structuring an argument addressing comparison, OR causation, OR change over time in explaining the environmental effects of networks of exchange. The reasoning used in the response might be uneven or imbalanced. Examples of using historical reasoning might include: • Byzantine and later Arab merchants transporting crops from India and China to the west. • The bubonic plague was transported west because of trade during the *Pax Mongolica*. • The Portuguese learned the pattern of currents in the Atlantic just as the Arabs had learned the monsoons.
Complexity (0-1 point)	Responses earn the complexity point by demonstrating a complex understanding of the environmental effects of networks of exchange. Ways of demonstrating a complex understanding of this prompt might include: • Explaining changes **AND** continuities, or similarities **AND** differences, or causes **AND** effects when describing the environmental effects of networks of exchange. • Describing the environmental effects of networks of exchange in another time period, for example during Columbian Exchange of 1500-1600.

Topics: 2.1, 2.3, 4, 2.6, 2.7

LEQ 4B Answer Key

Prompt: Develop an argument that evaluates the environmental effects of the Columbian Exchange in one or more regions during the period 1450-1750.

Point	Notes
Context (0-1 point)	Examples of context might include the following, with appropriate elaboration: • Explanation of the Age of Discovery and why European powers sought an alternative route to the East • Explanation of advancements in maritime technology
Thesis (0-1 point)	Responses earn one point by responding to the question with a historically defensible thesis that establishes a line of reasoning about the effects of the Columbian Exchange. Thesis statements need to demonstrate some degree of specificity regarding causation, OR comparison, OR change over time. Examples that earn this point include: • The Columbian Exchange improved nutrition in Europe and East Asia by introducing new American crops better suited to the environment. (comparison and causation) • Afro-Eurasian plants and domesticated animals were brought by Europeans to the Americas which had devastating environmental effects. (causation) • Populations in Afro-Eurasia benefitted nutritionally from the increased diversity of American food crops. (causation) • European colonization of the Americas led to the spread of diseases that were endemic in the Eastern Hemisphere, which substantially reduced the indigenous populations. (causation)
Evidence (0-2 points)	Responses earn one point by providing specific examples of evidence relevant to the topic of the prompt. Evidence used might include explanations of the following: • potato, corn, peanut, Ireland, smallpox, measles, and malaria, fruit trees, grains, sugar, horses Responses earn two points by using examples of specific historical evidence to support an argument in response to the prompt.
Reasoning (0-1 point)	Responses earn one point by framing or structuring an argument addressing causation, OR comparison, OR change over time in explaining the effects of the Columbian Exchange. The reasoning used in the response might be uneven or imbalanced. Examples of using historical reasoning might include: • A long-term effect of the Columbian Exchange is the destruction of the Native population which began with new diseases. • One change that occurred because of the Columbian Exchange was the introduction of plantation agriculture to the Americas, especially sugar plantations, which destroyed natural ecosystems
Complexity (0-1 point)	Responses earn the complexity point by demonstrating a complex understanding of the effects of the Columbian Exchange. Ways of demonstrating a complex understanding of this prompt might include: • Explaining changes **AND** continuities, or similarities **AND** differences, or causes **AND** effects when describing the effects of the Columbian Exchange. • Using comparison to show how the environmental effects of the Columbian Exchange were similar to the effects of exchange in another time period, for example comparing the diseases that decimated the Native Americans to the Bubonic Plague that decimated Europe and Asia in the previous time period.

Topics: 4.1, 4.2, 4.3, 4.4, 4.5, 4.8

LEQ 4C Answer Key

Prompt: Develop an argument that evaluates how human activity affected the environment in one or more regions during the period 1900-2001.

Point	Notes
Context (0-1 point)	Examples of context might include the following, with appropriate elaboration: • Explaining the rapid population growth after the Industrial Revolution • Explaining the rapid growth of technology that followed industrialization.
Thesis (0-1 point)	Responses earn one point by responding to the question with a historically defensible thesis that establishes a line of reasoning about how society affected the environment. Thesis statements need to demonstrate some degree of specificity regarding causation, OR comparison, OR change over time. Examples that earn this point include: • The greatest threat to the environment that faced society in the twentieth century was climate change which began slowly with industrialization but has steadily increased. (change over time) • In both Latin America and Asia improved agricultural technology has allowed for greater food production as part of the Green Revolution. (comparison and causation) • Human activity contributed to deforestation, desertification, a decline in air quality, and • increased consumption of the world's supply of fresh water. (causation)
Evidence (0-2 points)	Responses earn one point by providing specific examples of evidence relevant to the topic of the prompt. Evidence used might include explanations of the following: • Smog, oil spills, plastics, climate change, ozone, CO_2, man-made or naturally occurring, Green Revolution, GMOs, Indian Famine, new energy technologies, including the use of petroleum and nuclear power Responses earn two points by using examples of specific historical evidence to support an argument in response to the prompt.
Reasoning (0-1 point)	Responses earn one point by framing or structuring an argument addressing comparison, OR causation, OR change over time in explaining how society affected the environment. The reasoning used in the response might be uneven or imbalanced. Examples of using historical reasoning might include: • The release of greenhouse gases and pollutants into the atmosphere contributed to debates about the nature and causes of climate change. • In a consumer-based society everything is disposable, cell phones last a few years and are discarded, dumping tons of toxic chemicals into landfills. • As CO_2 builds up in the atmosphere, either naturally of from man-made sources, global temperatures rise. • Mexico and India are the two nations that benefited most from the Green Revolution.
Complexity (0-1 point)	Responses earn the complexity point by demonstrating a complex understanding of how society affected the environment. Ways of demonstrating a complex understanding of this prompt might include: • Explaining changes **AND** continuities, or similarities **AND** differences, or causes **AND** effects when describing how society affected the environment. • Use comparison to show how societies affected the environment during another time period, for example explaining the extreme pollution that occurred as nations industrialized during the previous time period.

Topics: 9.2, 9.3, 9.9

Made in the USA
Las Vegas, NV
09 November 2021